NOT
JUST
another
COOKBOOK

NOT
JUST
another
COOKBOOK

CLASSIC RECIPES, SIMPLE COOKING

COLLEEN G. BRETHEN

ORANGE *frazer* PRESS
Wilmington, Ohio

ISBN 9781939710-116

Published for Colleen Brethen by:
Orange Frazer Press
P.O. Box 214
Wilmington, OH 45177
Telephone: 800.852.9332 for price and shipping information.
Website: www.orangefrazer.com
www.orangefrazercustombooks.com

Colleen Brethen
40 North Main Street, Suite 2560
Dayton, Ohio 45423
www.notjustanothercookbook.com
937.671.4800

Book and cover design: Brittany Lament and Orange Frazer Press

Library of Congress Control Number 2014932645

Printed in China

I dedicate this book to my mother,
Frances Ramey, an amazing cook, and
to Joan Brethen, my mother-in-law,
whose wonderful recipe box was the
inspiration to write this book.

I think of you both every day.

TABLE OF CONTENTS

INTRODUCTION

Nothing beats the aroma of a home cooked meal and you don't have to be a chef to prepare one. This book is bursting with over 200 step-by-step, mouth-watering, tried and true recipes along with tips, techniques, nutritional facts, fascinating food and beverage history, famous food quotes, and bizarre trivia to entertain you.

Learn how to tell if an egg is fresh, how to peel tomatoes, or make the perfect soufflé. Offering a little something for everyone, this book helps a novice cook develop the confidence to prepare a full meal to entertain a crowd, while offering an experienced cook a challenge to create a masterpiece. There is something for everyone in this book and everybody will leave the table satisfied.

For those who cook only out of necessity or do not have an inclination to cook, you will be entertained by fun food facts like why you should eat your broccoli, read the interesting history behind how Crackerjacks got its name, and how Popeye and his creator were once credited for saving the spinach industry.

In the beginning, it all started with a discovery of an old recipe box filled with amazing old recipes I knew I had to share. The talk of writing a cookbook raised much enthusiasm from people I knew who wanted to contribute their favorite recipes. Others expressed interest in having a resource in helpful cooking tips, clarifications, and conversions while making it an interesting read.

I am grateful to those who have volunteered to help in the editing, illustrating, and photography. Also, I appreciate all the people who tasted the recipes with an objective palette. One thing is for sure, all recipes in this book are tried, true, and fabulous.

This book tries to keep things simple. Each recipe includes a timer with the information that will give you quick, "at a glance" ideas of what kind of time will be needed from preparation to serving. The box includes estimated times for preparation, marinating, microwaving, cooking, baking, broiling, grilling, chilling, set, or resting. It also includes the oven or grill temperatures, and the suggested serving sizes. The times are estimated and will vary based on your kitchen tools and equipment, altitude, interruptions and your culinary skills.

Example: PREP TIME: CHILL:
20 MINUTES   30 MINUTES

MAKES 2 CUPS

Many recipes include a "TIP" that makes alternative ingredient suggestions or comments. Although all the recipes are delicious and easy to put together as written, switching it up with similar ingredients or toppings can make a great alternative dish that will equally make a great crowd pleaser.

The last chapter, "Morsels & Tidbits," is the go-to chapter for a few basic cooking principles, clarifications, handy meat cooking time charts, and the ever so helpful ingredient equivalents and conversion charts.

Inside this book brews a wealth of amazing recipes full of flavor and goodness. No fancy decorations or garnishes needed; just classic recipes and simple cooking!

Enjoy!

NOT
JUST
another
COOKBOOK

CHAPTER ONE

A GREAT PLACE TO START
STARTERS, SNACKS, & TREATS

Appetizers didn't really catch on in America until well into the 20th Century. Some say finger foods evolved from bars that set out free food for their patrons. Another theory is that prohibition forced liquor out of the saloons and into the homes. Powered by all that bootlegged liquor and bathtub swill; bite size snacks were served to soak up all the booze.

After prohibition ended in 1933, the American cocktail party was born but was slow to gain in popularity. Guests, who were accustomed to eating food at a table, had to juggle bite-size nuggets on a napkin, hold their drink and maybe a cigarette, then mingle around the room.

The popularity of the cocktail party in America grew in the 1940s after the influence of James Beard, author of "Hors D'oeuvres and Canapés" (1940) introduced dips and cheese spreads. They became all the rage. Now guests could enjoy the simple "dunking" of vegetables or crackers into dips and soft spreads and still manage their drinks.

GUACAMOLE

MAKES 2 CUPS

PREP TIME: *10 MINUTES* CHILL: *30 MINUTES*

⅓ cup fresh cilantro, chopped
¼ cup red onion, minced
1 T jalapeño pepper, seeded, minced
3 avocados, halved, pitted, peeled
2 T fresh lime juice
kosher salt & black pepper to taste

Mix cilantro, onion, and jalapeño pepper in a non-reactive bowl. Roughly chop avocado flesh and spoon into onion mixture. Add lime juice and mash until smooth or to desired consistency. Add salt and pepper. Garnish with additional cilantro if desired. Chill for at least 30 minutes to allow flavors to blend.

TIP: *This guacamole recipe is a mild version. For more serious heat, add more jalapeño pepper or consider adding the seeds where most of the heat is stored. To keep the color bright green, place an avocado pit on top and store in an airtight container or cover with plastic wrap until ready to serve.*

JALAPEÑO POPPERS

MAKES 20 POPPERS

PREP TIME: *30 MINUTES* COOK: *20-30 MINUTES*

OVEN: GRILL OR 350°

1 T olive oil
1 medium onion, minced
¼ cup green pepper, minced
1 lb. bulk chorizo sausage
20 jalapeño peppers, seeded, cored
4 oz. Monterey jack cheese, grated

Sauté onion in olive oil over medium-high heat until onion is soft. Add sausage and cook for 5 to 7 minutes or until cooked through, crumbling the meat with a wooden spoon. Transfer meat to a paper towel-lined plate and let cool.

In a small bowl, combine the chorizo mixture and cheese. Stuff the center of each pepper with about 1 tablespoon of the mixture. Place in a pepper roaster or grill pan. Grill over indirect heat or bake on a baking sheet at 350° for 20 to 30 minutes.

TRY THIS!
To make this appetizer go a little faster, cut the jalapeño peppers in half lengthwise. Mound about 1 tablespoon of the mixture in each half, place on a baking sheet and bake in 350° oven for 20 minutes.

PREP TIME: 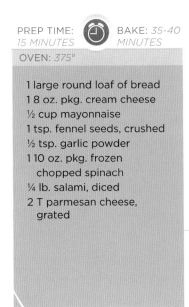 BAKE: *35-40*
15 MINUTES   *MINUTES*
OVEN: *375°*

1 large round loaf of bread
1 8 oz. pkg. cream cheese
½ cup mayonnaise
1 tsp. fennel seeds, crushed
½ tsp. garlic powder
1 10 oz. pkg. frozen
   chopped spinach
¼ lb. salami, diced
2 T parmesan cheese,
   grated

HOT SPINACH ROUND

MAKES 2 CUPS

Horizontally slice off top ¼ of bread loaf. Cut slice into 1-inch cubes. Cut vertically into center of loaf keeping 1-inch away from all sides. Lift center out and cut into 1-inch cubes; set loaf and cubes aside.

In a small bowl, combine cream cheese, mayonnaise, fennel seed, and garlic powder. Thaw spinach and place between paper towels to drain excess water. Add spinach and salami to cheese mixture.

Pour cheese mixture into bread round then sprinkle top with parmesan cheese. Bake uncovered, at 375° for 25 to 30 minutes. Lay out bread cubes in a single layer onto a baking sheet; bake at 375° for 10 minutes. Serve hot spinach round on a platter surrounded by bread cubes.

"I EATS ME SPINACH"

In 1937, Crystal City, Texas, erected a statue to honor both car-
toonist E. C. Segar and his famous character, Popeye, for their
influence on America's consumption of spinach. Popeye was
credited for a whopping 33% increase in sales and was given
recognition for single handedly saving the spinach industry.
—101 Foods

"I yam what I yam, and that's all what I yam."

SHRIMP DIP

MAKES 6 CUPS

In a large saucepan, dissolve gelatin in water. Stir in soup and cream cheese; heat until cheese is melted. Remove from heat and add remaining ingredients; mix thoroughly. Pour into mold or large bowl and refrigerate to firm for 6 hours or overnight. Un-mold onto a platter, garnish if desired and serve with crackers.

"Shrimp is the fruit of the sea. You can barbecue it, boil it, broil it, bake it, sauté it. There's, um, shrimp kebabs, shrimp creole, shrimp gumbo, pan fried, deep fried, stir fried. There's pineapple shrimp and lemon shrimp, coconut shrimp, pepper shrimp, shrimp soup, shrimp stew, shrimp salad, shrimp and potatoes, shrimp burger, shrimp sandwich... That's, that's about it." —Bubba Blue, Forrest Gump

PREP TIME: 30 MINUTES   CHILL: 6 HOURS

1 envelope unflavored gelatin
3 T water
1 10¾ oz. can cream of mushroom soup
1 8 oz. pkg. cream cheese
1 cup mayonnaise
1 4 oz. can tiny shrimp, minced
1 cup celery, minced
1 cup green pepper, minced
1 cup green onion, minced

SHRIMP SALSA

MAKES 3 CUPS

Combine shrimp, onion, cilantro, tomato, jalapeño, cheese, and avocado in a medium bowl. In a separate bowl, whisk together lime juice, oil, salt, and pepper. Toss with shrimp mixture. Cover and refrigerate to allow flavors to blend for about 4 hours. Serve with tortilla chips.

PREP TIME: 30 MINUTES   CHILL: 4 HOURS

1 lb. large shrimp, cooked, chopped
¼ cup red onion, minced
¼ cup cilantro, chopped
1 Roma tomato, seeded, diced
1 to 2 tsp. jalapeño peppers, minced
3 oz. feta cheese, crumbled
2 avocados, diced
2 T fresh lime juice
2 T olive oil
1 tsp. kosher salt
½ tsp. black pepper
tortilla chips

PREP TIME: CHILL:
30 MINUTES   *4 HOURS*

1 6 oz. can pink salmon,
  drained, picked through,
  flaked
1 8 oz. pkg. cream cheese
1½ T fresh lemon juice
1½ T low-fat milk
1 tsp. fresh dill weed
2 T green onions, thinly
  sliced
2 drops Liquid Smoke
toasted French bread or
  crackers

SMOKEY SALMON SPREAD

MAKES 3 CUPS

Beat together all ingredients until well combined. Chill for 4 hours before serving to allow the flavors to blend.

NOT JUST A FISH TALE
In the late 1800s a chemist named, Earnest Wright, noticed a black liquid dripping from his stove pipe. After much pondering, he developed a method to capture that smell of smoke as it passed through water. The new "condensed smoke" liquid flavoring is now commonly known as the product, Liquid Smoke.
—Wikipedia

GOOD TO KNOW
Salmon is rich in omega-3 fatty acids, which helps in proper brain function and a healthy cardiovascular system. —101 Foods

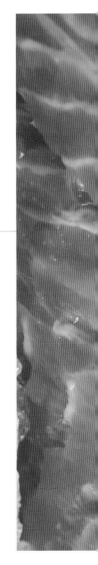

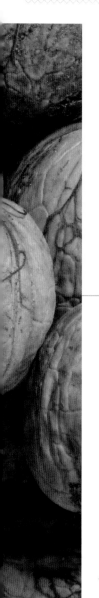

APPLE CHEDDAR & WALNUT TOASTS

PREP TIME:
15 MINUTES

BROIL:
6-7 MINUTES

24 thin slices of narrow
French bread

2 tart apples, cored, thinly
sliced

8 oz. extra sharp cheddar
cheese, finely shredded

1 cup walnuts, roughly
chopped

MAKES 24 TOASTS

Arrange bread on a baking sheet and toast lightly on both sides under broiler, about 1 minute each side. Place 2 apple slices on each toast, mound cheese on top and press walnut pieces into cheese. Broil about 4 to 5 inches below broiler for 4 to 5 minutes or until cheese melts and walnuts are lightly colored.

"APPLE POLISHER"

The old custom of "apple polishing" hails from the little red schoolhouses of yore. Young children whose math skills were less than exemplary sought to win their teacher's favor instead with a gift of a bright, shiny apple. Remember this ditty? "An apple for the teacher will always do the trick when you don't know your lesson in arithmetic."
—USApple.org

PREP TIME: BAKE:
30 MINUTES   *16 MINUTES*

OVEN: *400°*

8 oz. shrimp, cooked, diced
2 T feta cheese, crumbled
½ cup white rice, cooked,
    tightly packed
½ cup diced tomatoes,
    drained
¼ tsp. dried oregano
½ tsp. kosher salt, divided
½ tsp. black pepper, divided
12 egg roll wrappers

GREEK EGG ROLLS

SERVES 6

In a medium bowl, combine shrimp, cheese, rice, tomatoes, oregano and ¼ teaspoon of each salt and pepper; mix well. Place an egg roll wrapper on a flat surface with corners pointing up. Place 3 tablespoons of shrimp filling just below center of wrapping. Fold bottom over filling packing the filling in tightly. Fold in sides and roll to top. Seal any loose ends by lightly brushing with water. Repeat with remaining ingredients. Place filled wrappers on a lightly greased baking sheet. Spray lightly with cooking spray. Bake at 400° for 16 minutes, flipping once or until golden brown.

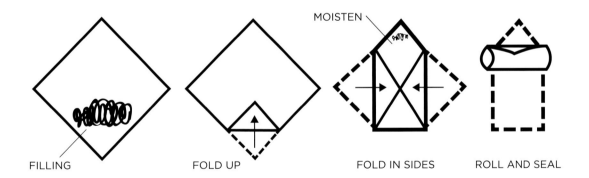

FILLING   FOLD UP   MOISTEN   FOLD IN SIDES   ROLL AND SEAL

YANKEE REVENGE PINWHEELS

MAKES 5 DOZEN

PREP TIME:
15 MINUTES

CHILL:
*2 HOURS-
OVERNIGHT*

- 3 8 oz. pkgs. cream cheese
- 10 green onions, chopped with tops
- 1 T fresh lime juice
- 1 T medium hot picante sauce
- 1 to 2 jalapeño peppers, diced
- ½ tsp. Tabasco hot pepper sauce
- 1 25 oz. pkg. large flour tortillas (10 tortillas)

Mix all ingredients; spread on tortillas, roll up tightly, wrap in foil and refrigerate 2 hours to overnight. Cut into ¼ inch thick slices and serve with picante sauce.

"Yankee Doodle came to town
Riding on a pony
Stuck a feather in his cap and
Called it macaroni"

This well-known nursery rhyme is not so innocent. British officers of the Revolutionary War sang the song in mockery of the poorly dressed and disorganized New Englanders. The term "doodle" meant fool or simpleton and although "macaroni" was an extremely fashionable wig worn in the 1770s, it became slang for someone who was foolishly concerned with fashion or with their appearance.

The tune was still in favor during the Civil War. Ulysses S. Grant once said "I only know two tunes: one of them is "Yankee Doodle," and the other one isn't."

PREP TIME: COOK:
5 MINUTES   *10 MINUTES*
SET: *1 TO 2 WEEKS*

1 dozen eggs, hard boiled
½ tsp. kosher salt
½ tsp. Accent flavor
   enhancer
2 bay leaves
¼ tsp. ground ginger
1 Serrano pepper, julienned
2 cloves garlic, halved
2½ cups distilled white
   vinegar
2½ cups water
1 T hot pepper sauce
   (optional)

HOT PICKLED EGGS

MAKES 1 DOZEN

Put eggs in a 2 quart pickle jar or airtight container. Combine all remaining ingredients in a large sauce pan. Boil on medium heat for 10 minutes; remove from heat and slightly cool.

Pour vinegar solution over eggs, seal jar and refrigerate. Set for 1 week for small eggs and 2 weeks for medium to large eggs before eating. Use eggs within 3 to 4 months for best quality. Texas Pete hot pepper sauce works well with this recipe. You might even add a few of the peppers in for more heat.

TIPS FOR HARD BOILING EGGS

• *To prevent cracking, start with eggs covered in 1 to 2 inches of cold water and gently bring to a boil.*

• *Salt also helps prevent cracking but do not add until water is hot or you may cause "pitting" damage to the bottom of your pot.*

• *Adding 1 tablespoon of vinegar to the water will help keep egg whites from running out of a cracked shell.*

• *Adding a few drops of food coloring into the water will help distinguish the hard boiled eggs from the raw.*

BUFFALO WINGS

PREP TIME: 15 MINUTES   MARINATE: 30 MINUTES

BROIL: 20 MINUTES

2 lbs. chicken wings (about 12 wings)
3 T butter, melted
4 T hot pepper sauce
1 T paprika
½ tsp. kosher salt
½ tsp. cayenne pepper
¼ tsp. black pepper

SERVES 4-6

Cut off chicken wing tips, cut wings at the joint, wash and pat dry. Place chicken pieces in a plastic bag; set aside. Combine butter, hot pepper sauce, paprika, salt, cayenne, and black pepper. Pour all but 2 tablespoons of marinade over the chicken pieces in the bag. Seal bag and marinate 30 minutes in refrigerator. Drain and discard marinade.

Place wing pieces on a broiler pan. Broil 4 to 5 inches from heat for about 10 minutes each side. Baste with remaining marinade before serving.

TIP: *Use Crystal, Franks Original, or Louisiana hot pepper sauce. The wings taste great served with the Blue Cheese Dip recipe on page 13.*

RUMOR HAS IT
There is some question about who came up with the original buffalo wing appetizer, but most credit the Anchor Bar in where else but Buffalo, New York, USA on October 30, 1964.
—Wikipedia

PREP TIME: CHILL:
5 MINUTES   1-2 HOURS

½ cup sour cream
½ cup blue cheese, crumbled
½ cup mayonnaise
1 T white wine vinegar or white vinegar
1 clove garlic, minced

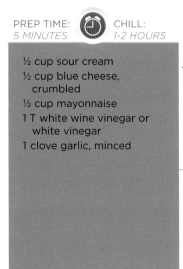

BLUE CHEESE DIP

MAKES 1½ CUPS

Combine sour cream, blue cheese, mayonnaise, vinegar, and garlic; mix well. Cover and refrigerate for 1 to 2 hours to allow the flavors to blend. Store dip in an airtight container for up to 1 week.

FOOD FOR THOUGHT

While an obvious pairing with blue cheese dip may be Buffalo wings, the natural salty taste of blue cheese offers a savory compliment when drizzled over a steak or on a hamburger. Give it a try!

PREP TIME: CHILL:
15 MINUTES   2 HOURS

1 14 oz. can diced tomatoes
1 10 oz. can Rotel tomatoes (original)
juice of 1 lime
1 cup onion, roughly chopped
¼ cup cilantro, clean, pat dry, roughly chopped
1 clove garlic, minced
1 jalapeno, seeded, roughly chopped
1 tsp. honey
½ tsp. kosher salt
¼ tsp. ground cumin

SIMPLE SALSA

MAKES 4 CUPS

Put all ingredients in a food processor or blender. Pulse for 30 seconds or to desired consistency. Cover and refrigerate for at least 2 hours to allow flavors to blend. Salsa can be stored in an airtight container in the refrigerator for up to 1 week.

TIP: *This is a mild salsa recipe. For a more serious heat, add more jalapeno or add the seeds where most of the heat is stored.*

LOLLIPOPS & HARD CANDY

PREP TIME: 5 MINUTES   COOK: 20-30 MINUTES

2 cups granulated sugar
⅔ cups light corn syrup
¾ cup water
1 dram (1 tsp.) flavoring
food coloring as needed
powdered sugar (optional)

MAKES ABOUT 3 CUPS

In a large saucepan, mix together sugar, corn syrup, and water. Stir over medium heat until sugar dissolves. Bring mixture to a boil without stirring. Add color when syrup reaches 260°. Do not stir; boiling action will incorporate the color into the syrup.

Remove hot syrup from heat at 300° or when drops of syrup form hard brittle threads in cold water. After boiling action ceases, add flavoring and stir. Pour syrup into lightly oiled candy molds or onto a greased sheet pan and score to mark squares. When cool, remove from molds or break into pieces. Dust with powdered sugar.

WARNING!
Use extreme caution while working with the hot sugar syrup. Severe burns can occur if the syrup touches your skin.

CANDIED APPLES

PREP TIME: 5 MINUTES   COOK: 20 MINUTES
SET: 20 MINUTES

6 to 8 small red apples
6 to 8 wooden skewers
1½ cups sugar
½ cup light corn syrup
½ cup water
dash of salt
½ tsp. red coloring
½ tsp. vanilla or candy flavoring

MAKES 6-8 APPLES

Boil each apple for 15 seconds and carefully wipe wax coating off of hot apples. Insert a wooden skewer in the stem of each apple. Combine and cook sugar, syrup, water, and salt over low heat until sugar is dissolved. Boil without stirring to the light crack stage or about 290°. Remove from heat; blend in food coloring and vanilla. Quickly dip apples into hot syrup, twirling to coat evenly. Stand upright on a greased baking sheet or parchment paper to cool.

WARNING!
Use extreme caution while working with the hot sugar syrup. Severe burns can occur if the syrup touches your skin.

PREP TIME: BAKE:
5 MINUTES   *1 HOUR*

MICRO: *5 MINUTES* OVEN: *250°*

- 12 cups popped corn
- 1 cup mini pretzels
- 1 cup salted cashews
- 1 large paper grocery bag
- ½ cup unsalted butter (1 stick)
- ½ cup unsalted brown sugar, packed
- ¼ cup light corn syrup
- ½ tsp. salt
- ½ tsp. baking soda

CARAMEL CORN

MAKES 14 CUPS

Place popped corn, pretzels, and cashews into paper bag; shake to combine. Melt butter in a large microwave-safe bowl for 1 minute. Stir in brown sugar, corn syrup, and salt. Microwave 2 minutes (the mixture will boil). Carefully stir mixture and microwave for another 2 minutes. Stir in baking soda (it will foam up).

Pour butter mixture over popcorn mixture in bag. Fold top of bag and shake mixture well to coat popcorn. Transfer mixture onto a lightly greased sheet pan and bake at 250° for 1 hour stirring occasionally. Break up clumps as it cools.

THAT'S CRACKERJACK!

In 1893, Norman and Louis Altman sold popcorn and peanuts mixed together with molasses at the Chicago World's Fair. They called it "Candied Popcorn and Peanuts." Although it was a big hit, there was also a big problem; the popcorn and peanuts stuck together in clusters.

Three years later they devised a way to keep the kernels separate. Each batch was mixed in a cement-mixer type drum with a small amount of oil added in. One enthusiastic sampler remarked "That's crackerjack!" (The colloquialism meaning: "of excellent quality.") Hence the origin of the famous treat's name Crackerjacks.

SPICY CHICKPEAS

MAKES 1½ CUPS

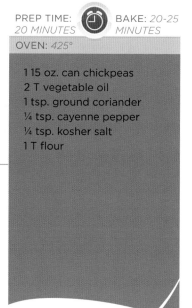

PREP TIME: 20 MINUTES
BAKE: 20-25 MINUTES
OVEN: 425°

1 15 oz. can chickpeas
2 T vegetable oil
1 tsp. ground coriander
¼ tsp. cayenne pepper
¼ tsp. kosher salt
1 T flour

Rinse and drain chickpeas well. Toss peas in oil, coriander, cayenne pepper, and salt, then toss with flour. Spread coated peas on a lightly greased baking sheet. Bake at 425°, stirring once for 20 to 25 minutes or until golden. Cool on paper towels.

TIP: *Also known as garbanzo beans, chickpeas are a great source of protein. But be careful; they are also high in carbs. This recipe makes a great snack and also makes an excellent salad topping.*

SPICED NUTS

MAKES 3 CUPS

PREP TIME: 20 MINUTES
BAKE: 20-25 MINUTES
OVEN: 325°

1 egg white
2 tsp. water
1 T sugar
1 tsp. ground cinnamon
¼ tsp. salt
¼ tsp. cayenne pepper
¼ tsp. coriander
¼ tsp. cumin
3 cups almonds or mixed nuts

In a medium bowl, beat egg white with water until frothy. Add all seasonings; beat to combine. Stir in nuts; toss to coat evenly.

Spread nut mixture onto a lightly greased baking pan. Bake at 325° for 20 to 25 minutes or until golden and nuts appear to be dry.

Cool on paper towels, breaking apart large clusters. Store spiced nuts in an airtight container at room temperature for up to 1 week.

A whole book could be written on the many causes and cures for a hangover. Many suggestions I found were based more on old wives tales than proven medical research. A good example is having "a bit of the hair of the dog that bit you."

Drinking a Bloody Mary when you wake with a hangover is probably not a good idea. Try a Virgin Mary instead. The tomato juice with a celery garnish is full of helpful vitamins. Here are a few other helpful tips to prevent or cure a hangover.

GEARING UP TO PARTY—Start by eating a good meal high in fat. It digests slowly, protecting the stomach from the effects of alcohol. Eat or drink something fruity for added nutrition and drink plenty of water to get your body hydrated.

CHAPTER TWO

I'LL HAVE ANOTHER!
ADULT BEVERAGES & REFRESHMENTS

DURING THE PARTY—Stick to the same drink and drink a glass of water in between each alcoholic beverage.

BEFORE PASSING OUT—Alcohol robs the body of essential vitamins and minerals, so it's a good idea to take vitamins, especially vitamin-B before retiring. Add more fat before you go to bed with a tall glass of milk. Do not take acetaminophen or aspirin. Effects can be magnified when mixed with alcohol and they may cause liver damage or stomach bleeding.

THE MORNING AFTER—Get up and move; activate your body. Taking a shower switching between hot and cold may help. You may not feel like eating but it's the best way to help your body recover. Eggs have amino acid cysteine that helps the liver recover from the stress of breaking down alcohol. Eat foods high in minerals and proteins. Try eating bananas, fish, pickles, and even drink a little pickle juice. Alcohol can deplete sugar levels so eating some carbs may make you feel better.

BRANDY STYLE KAHLUA
TRADITIONAL KAHLUA
RUSSIAN TEA
BASIC MARGARITA
MARGA-BEER-ITAS
PAIN KILLER
RASBERRY-MANGO SANGRIA
WHISKEY PUNCH
TANGERINE SPARKLERS
HOT MULLED CIDER
ICED COFFEE
AMARETTO NOG
IRISH CREAM

BRANDY STYLE KAHLUA

PREP TIME: *15 MINUTES*   COOK: *10 MINUTES*

SET: *3 WEEKS*

2 cups water
2 cups white sugar
½ cup instant coffee (not freeze dried)
1½ cups 80 proof brandy
½ vanilla bean, sliced crosswise into ½" pieces

MAKES 4 CUPS

Boil sugar in water, stirring constantly, for 10 minutes or until sugar has completely dissolved. Turn off heat, slowly add instant coffee and continue to stir until blended; set aside to cool completely.

Combine brandy with vanilla bean pieces; add to coffee mixture. Pour into air tight jars or containers, evenly distributing vanilla bean pieces between containers. Cover and shake vigorously each day for 3 weeks. Strain to remove vanilla bean pieces and seeds before drinking.

TIP: *This is a great holiday gift idea. You can find inexpensive glass bottles online. I ordered mine at www.specialtybottle.com.*

PREP TIME: *15 MINUTES*
BAKE: *10 MINUTES*
SET: *3 WEEKS*

4 cups water
4 cups sugar
½ cup instant coffee (not freeze dried)
1 750 ml. bottle 100 proof vodka
1 vanilla bean, sliced crosswise into ½" pieces

TRADITIONAL KAHLUA

MAKES 12 CUPS

Boil sugar in water, stirring constantly, for 10 minutes or until sugar has completely dissolved. Turn off heat, slowly add instant coffee and continue to stir until blended; set aside to cool completely. Combine vodka and vanilla bean; add to the coffee mixture.

Pour into air tight jars or containers, evenly distributing vanilla bean pieces between containers. Cover and shake vigorously each day for 3 weeks. Strain to remove vanilla bean pieces and seeds before drinking.

TIP: *Chocolate flavored coffee works well and you can also try French vanilla or a hazelnut blend. Kahlua does not need refrigeration but if the consistency is thin, try storing it in the freezer.*

PREP TIME: *15 MINUTES*

2 cups Tang drink mix
5 oz. instant lemonade
¼ cup instant tea powder
¾ cup lemon flavored instant tea powder
1 tsp. ground cinnamon
½ tsp. ground cloves
1 cup sugar (optional)

RUSSIAN TEA

MAKES 100 SERVINGS

Combine all ingredients, mixing well. Mix 3 teaspoons per 8 ounce cup of hot water or to taste.

TIP: *This is an inexpensive and great tasting recipe to make for holiday gifts.*

BASIC MARGARITA

2 MINUTES

2 oz. 100% agave tequila
1 oz. fresh lime juice
1 oz. agave nectar or to taste
1 oz. water

MAKES 1 SERVING

Squeeze limes with a hand juicer, screening out any pulp. Combine all ingredients into a shaker with ice. Give it a good shake and pour into the glass, no need for new ice.

TIP: *Out of the countless margarita recipes out there, I like this recipe because it's made with fresh lime juice and is so simple to make. Even after your 4th or 5th drink you should remember the mix … Well, okay maybe not.*

MARGA-BEER-ITAS

PREP TIME:
2 MINUTES

6 to 8 small red apples
1 12 oz. can lime juice
   frozen concentrate
1 12 oz. can of beer, cold
1 12 oz. can lemon lime
   soda, cold
12 oz. Jose Cuervo gold
   tequila

MAKES 4-6 SERVINGS

Combine all ingredients in a pitcher.
Stir and serve.

TIP: *What's great about this simple margarita recipe is you can keep all the ingredients on hand for that sudden urge to have a fiesta. Ole!*

PREP TIME:
2 MINUTES

1 cup of ice
2 oz. dark rum
2 oz. cream of coconut
3 oz. pineapple juice
2 oz. fresh orange juice
sprinkle of nutmeg
1 maraschino cherry
  (optional)

TRY THIS!
*Pusser's rum and
Coco Lopez cream
of coconut is
recommended.*

PAIN KILLER

MAKES 1 SERVING

Fill a glass with ice. Pour rum over ice. Add cream of coconut, pineapple juice, and orange juice; shake well. Top with cherry and a sprinkle of nutmeg.

RUMOR ALERT

The Soggy Dollar Bar on the island of Jost Van Dyke in the British Virgin Islands stakes a claim to have originated and perfected the Pain Killer cocktail. As they say at the Soggy Dollar, "it's a sunny drink for shady people." —Wikipedia, soggydollar.com

PREP TIME:
5 MINUTES

CHILL:
1 HOUR

1 mango, peeled, pitted,
  thinly sliced lengthwise
1 cup raspberries
3 T raspberry liqueur
1 750 ml bottle rose wine
4 cups (32 oz.) lemon-lime
  soda, chilled
ice

RASPBERRY-MANGO SANGRIA

MAKES 8 SERVINGS

Combine mango, raspberries, raspberry liqueur, and rose wine in a pitcher. Refrigerate at least 1 hour or up to overnight. To serve, add lemon-lime soda and ice.

TIP: *If you cannot find ripe mangos or raspberries, no worries, there are countless combinations of fruit that pair well together. Strawberries, kiwis, melons, grapes, and any citrus fruit will work great.*

WHISKEY PUNCH

MAKES 16 SERVINGS

1 cup sugar syrup (see below)

4 cups strong black tea

1 12 oz. can lemon juice frozen concentrate

1 2 qt. bottle lemon lime soda

1 750 ml. bottle whiskey

Mix all ingredients thoroughly. Pour over ice and serve.

SUGAR SYRUP: *Mix 2 cups of sugar to 1 cup of water. Bring to a boil stirring constantly until sugar is completely dissolved and liquid is clear.*

GOOD TO KNOW

An unopened bottle of whiskey can keep 100 years and still be good to drink. After opening, however, a half bottle will last only about 5 years. So, drink up!

If you ever find yourself in an Irish pub, you might hear the words "Uisce Beatha" (whiskey), which translates from Gaelic as the "Water of Life."

Whiskey and food have long been a complement for each other. Some commonly known recipes that include whiskey are bourbon chicken, chicken breasts in Irish cream, and the Asian dish, drunken chicken. It's also used in many popular barbecue sauces. Also, try pairing whiskey with chocolate, cheese, apples or pears.

TANGERINE SPARKLERS

MAKES 8 SERVINGS

ice, cubed & crushed

2 cups orange-tangerine juice

3 cups seltzer or ginger ale

tangerine or orange slices

In a large chilled pitcher filled with ice cubes, combine the juice and seltzer. Pour mixture into chilled glasses filled with crushed ice. Garnish with fruit slices.

PREP TIME:    COOK:
5 MINUTES   2-10 HOURS

2 quarts apple cider
½ cup light brown sugar
2 cinnamon sticks
1½ tsp. whole cloves
1 tsp. whole allspice
1 orange, thinly sliced

HOT MULLED CIDER

MAKES 8-10 SERVINGS

Put all ingredients in a slow cooker. If desired, tie the whole spices in cheesecloth or a tea strainer. Cover and cook on low for 2 to 10 hours. Serve hot.

TIP: *Make spiced wine using the same recipe and substituting 2 750ml. bottles of sweet sherry or port in lieu of the apple cider.*

PREP TIME:    SET:
2 MINUTES   4 HOURS -
                         OVERNIGHT

¼ cup ground coffee
1½ cups cold water

ICED COFFEE

MAKES 1-2 SERVINGS

Combine coffee and water together in an air tight container; shake well until well blended. Refrigerate overnight or for at least 4 hours. Strain mixture through a coffee filter or fine mesh strainer. Add milk and/or sugar to taste.

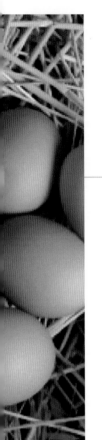

AMARETTO NOG

PREP TIME:
20 MINUTES

CHILL:
1 HOUR

1 cup frozen whipped topping, thawed
1 14 oz. can sweetened condensed milk
1 fresh egg
2 tsp. vanilla
½ 375 ml. bottle amaretto liqueur

MAKES 3 CUPS

Mix whipped topping and milk on low speed in a blender until smooth. Add in egg and vanilla then amaretto; combine thoroughly. Chill and serve.

THE BITTER TRUTH

Amaretto is often considered an almond liqueur but it may in fact, not have any almonds in it at all. Many amaretto recipes use apricot pits as the base ingredient.

It has been enjoyed in Italy for centuries, but it wasn't until the 1960s that the liqueur was imported to the United States. By the mid-1980s, amaretto was only second to Kahlua in liqueur sales. Amaretto is a diminutive of the Italian word, amaro, meaning "bitter." —About.com

IRISH CREAM

PREP TIME:
5 MINUTES

CHILL:
1 HOUR

1¾ cups Irish whiskey
1 14 oz. can sweetened condensed milk
1 cup whipping or light cream
4 fresh eggs
2 T chocolate syrup
2 tsp. instant coffee (not freeze dried)
1 tsp. vanilla extract
1 tsp. almond extract

MAKES 5 CUPS

Combine all ingredients in a blender until smooth. Chill. Store Irish cream in a covered container in refrigerator for up to 1 month. Stir or shake before serving.

AN OLD IRISH BLESSING

May the road rise up to meet you, may the wind be always at your back, may the sun shine warm upon your face, and the rain fall soft upon your fields, and until we meet again, may God, hold you in the palm of His hand.

BREAKING THE FAST

It's true! Breakfast is the most important meal of the day. The body breaks from fasting during the night, kick starts the metabolism (burning calories) into gear and sets the pace for the whole day. Studies have proven that weight loss is more difficult and weight gain is more prevalent when people skip breakfast. Here are a few reasons why:

• The body's metabolism burns food more readily after the morning meal and stays active through the day making it easier to digest all meals and maintain a healthy weight.

• If the body is starving it tries to hold on to the next meal for as long as it can, sometimes storing it right at the waistline.

CHAPTER THREE

THE MOST IMPORTANT MEAL
BREAKFASTS & FRUIT FARE

• When skipping breakfast, people tend to snack on any food available, often high-calorie foods just to keep the hunger at bay until lunch time.

• People missing breakfast tend to consume more than usual at the next meal because their blood sugar is low and they feel famished.

• Eating a good breakfast helps in controlling appetite and portion size of the next meal.

• People who skip breakfast often lack the fuel they need to fight off the foggy head, headaches, and bad attitudes.

According to the American Institute for Cancer Research, eating a healthy breakfast of fruits and vegetables, along with regular exercise and maintaining a healthy weight, can reduce the risk of cancer.

BLUEBERRY MUFFINS

MAKES 10 MUFFINS

PREP TIME: 15 MINUTES

BAKE: 23-25 MINUTES
OVEN: 375°

2 cups all-purpose flour
¾ cup + 5 tsps. sugar, divided
¾ tsp. baking powder
½ tsp. baking soda
½ tsp. salt
½ cup milk
2 eggs
½ cup vegetable oil
1 tsp. grated orange zest
1 cup fresh blueberries

Coat a muffin pan with non-stick cooking spray or use paper liners; set aside. In a large bowl whisk flour, ¾ cup sugar, baking powder, baking soda, and salt. Make a well in the center of bowl; set aside.

In a small bowl, whisk together milk, eggs, oil, and orange zest. Pour milk mixture into well of dry ingredients then stir just until combined; fold in blueberries. Pour about ⅓ cup of batter into each muffin cup. Fill the 2 empty muffin cups with water so the muffins bake evenly. Sprinkle each muffin with ½ teaspoon of sugar. Bake at 375° for 23 to 25 minutes, until crowned and lightly brown. Cool muffins on a rack.

TRUE BLUE

Blueberries have been used for more than a healthy breakfast fruit. Early American colonists made grey paint by boiling blueberries in milk. The Shakers made blue paint from sage blossoms, indigo, blueberry skins, and milk using it primarily in painting their woodwork. —Foodreference.com

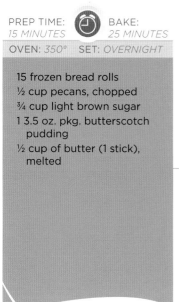

PREP TIME: *15 MINUTES*   BAKE: *25 MINUTES*

OVEN: *350°*   SET: *OVERNIGHT*

- 15 frozen bread rolls
- ½ cup pecans, chopped
- ¾ cup light brown sugar
- 1 3.5 oz. pkg. butterscotch pudding
- ½ cup of butter (1 stick), melted

PREP TIME: *5 MINUTES*   BAKE: *15 MINUTES*

OVEN: *350°*   COOK: *3 MINUTES*

- 2 peaches, peeled, pitted, halved
- 1½ T brown sugar
- ¼ tsp. ground cinnamon
- 3 T butter
- ⅓ cup granola

MONKEY BREAD

MAKES 6-8 SERVINGS

Put pecans in bottom of a bundt pan. Add rolls, placing evenly around pan. Sprinkle brown sugar on top then sprinkle butterscotch pudding over sugar. Pour butter over top, cover lightly and let rise overnight. Bake at 350° for 25 minutes. Turn over onto a platter and serve.

BAKED PEACHES

MAKES 4 SERVINGS

Place peaches cut side up on an 18 inch piece of aluminum foil. Combine brown sugar with cinnamon and sprinkle on center of each peach half. Put about 1 teaspoon of butter in each half. Fold foil over peaches and loosely seal. Place peaches on grill over moderate heat or in oven at 350° for 15 minutes.

Meanwhile, melt remaining butter in a small saucepan and stir in granola. Cook for about 2 to 3 minutes or until granola is well coated. Serve peaches on a platter topped with a sprinkling of granola.

TIP: *Peaches are a summer fruit peaking in July. While it's hard to replicate the sweetness of a fresh peach, a good off-season pick is Del Monte Freestone Peaches in a can. Del Monte hand picks their peaches and starts the canning process right away during the harvest season.*

MINI FRITTATAS

½ lb. thin ham slices (6 large slices)
1 T vegetable oil
1 cup potato, peeled, diced
½ cup onion, minced
½ cup red bell pepper, minced
kosher salt & pepper to taste
8 large eggs
6 T milk

MAKES 6 SERVINGS

Preheat oven to 375°. Lightly grease a 12 cup muffin pan. Cut each ham slice in half and press into each muffin cup; set aside.

Heat oil in a skillet over medium-high heat. Cook potatoes until softened and golden, about 5 minutes. Add onion and bell pepper; continue to cook for 3 to 5 minutes. Season with salt and divide mixture among the muffin cups.

Whisk together eggs and milk and pour into muffin cups so that each cup is about half full. Bake until eggs are cooked through, about 15 minutes. Let stand for 5 minutes, remove frittatas from pan and serve warm.

TIP: *A frittata is an open faced omelet and much like a quiche where the ingredients are mixed into the egg rather than used as a filling. This easy and delicious recipe tastes great served with a breakfast steak or pork chops.*

Easy and delicious!

PREP TIME: 25 MINUTES   BAKE: *30-35 MINUTES*

OVEN: *350°*   RAISE: *5-8 HOURS*

- 2 1 lb. frozen bread loaves
- ½ lb. mild pork sausage
- ½ lb. hot pork sausage
- ½ cup onion, chopped
- 1½ cups mushrooms, diced
- 1 tsp. dried basil
- 1 tsp. dried parsley
- 1 tsp. dried rosemary, crushed
- 1 tsp. garlic powder
- 3 eggs, divided
- 2 cups Mozzarella cheese, shredded

BREAKFAST SAUSAGE LOAVES

MAKES 8 SERVINGS

Thaw and allow dough to rise until nearly doubled, about 5 to 8 hours. Cook both sausages in a skillet over medium heat, chopping to crumble into small pieces. Add in onion, mushrooms, and all seasonings. Continue to cook until sausage is brown and onion is tender; drain and cool. Beat 2 eggs and combine with sausage mixture and cheese.

On a floured surface, roll each loaf of dough into a 12" x 16" rectangle. Spread half the sausage mixture on each loaf to within 1 inch of edges. Roll jelly-roll style, starting at narrow end; seal edges. Place on a greased baking sheet. Bake at 350° for 25 minutes. Beat remaining egg and brush on loaves. Bake 5 to 10 minutes more or until golden brown.

Golden brown!

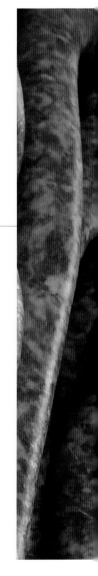

FARMER'S STRATA

PREP TIME: 15 MINUTES

BAKE: *65-70 MINUTES*

OVEN: *325°* SET: *30 MINUTES*

1 lb. bacon, cut into ½" pieces
2 cups cooked ham, chopped
1 small onion, chopped
10 slices white bread, cubed
1 cup potatoes, cooked, cubed
3 cups cheddar cheese, shredded
8 eggs
3 cups milk
1 T Worcestershire sauce
1 tsp. dry mustard
pinch of kosher salt & black pepper

MAKES 10 SERVINGS

Cook bacon in a skillet until crisp. Add ham and onion. Continue to cook until onion is tender; drain. In a greased 13" x 9" baking dish, layer half the bread, potatoes, and cheese. Top with bacon mixture. Repeat layers.

In a medium bowl, beat eggs, milk, Worcestershire sauce, mustard, salt, and pepper. Pour over layers in baking dish; cover and refrigerate overnight. Remove from refrigerator 30 minutes before baking. Bake at 325° uncovered, about 70 minutes or until a knife comes out clean.

HOW TO TELL IF EGGS ARE FRESH
• *Fill a deep bowl with cold tap water then gently drop an egg into the water.*
• *If it sinks to the bottom and stays there, it's about 3 to 6 days old and is fresh.*
• *Sinks, but floats at an angle, it's more than 1 week old; still good but not as fresh.*
• *Sinks, but then stands on end, it's about 2 weeks old; old but still edible.*
• *If the egg floats, it's too old and should be discarded.*

PREP TIME: 15 MINUTES
BAKE: 75 MINUTES
OVEN: 300° CHILL: OVERNIGHT

8 slices sourdough bread, cubed
2 cups sharp cheddar cheese, shredded
1 lb. bulk mild sausage
4 eggs
3 cups milk, divided
¾ tsp. dry mustard
1 10¾ oz. can cream of mushroom soup

BREAKFAST CASSEROLE

MAKES 8-10 SERVINGS

Place bread cubes in the bottom of a greased 9" x 13" baking dish. Top with cheese. Brown sausage; drain off fat, then scatter on top of cheese. Beat eggs, 2½ cups of milk, and dry mustard together until well combined. Pour over top, cover and refrigerate overnight.

Dilute soup with the remaining ½ cup of milk and pour over casserole. Bake uncovered at 300° for 1 hour and 15 minutes.

SOURDOUGH STARTERS

A sourdough "starter" is a ball of dough made from flour and water. Also known as unleavened dough, it is used as a medium to grow yeast. It begins to "sour" as it goes through a fermentation process, eventually becoming leavened dough.

In the Gold Rush days of the late 1800s, prospectors, miners, mountain men, and pioneers of the Old West were often referred to as "Sourdoughs" because they would carry a sourdough starter with them from camp to camp. They would protect the dough ball by placing it within a sack of flour and would even take it to bed with them to keep the cold night air from stopping the crucial fermentation process. —Foodreference.com

APPLESAUCE

PREP TIME:
5 MINUTES

COOK: *15-20 MINUTES*

CHILL: *30 MINUTES*

4 medium apples, peeled, cored, quartered
¾ cup water
¼ cup brown or white sugar
¼ tsp. ground cinnamon (optional)

MAKES 2 CUPS

Combine apples, water, sugar, and cinnamon in a large saucepan. Cover and cook over medium heat for 15 to 20 minutes. Drain apples, reserving juice and let cool to touch.

Mash cooked apples with a fork or puree in a food processor. Add in reserved juice, one spoonful at a time, until you reach the right consistency and sweetness. Chill for about 30 minutes before serving.

AN APPLE A DAY...

That well-known saying "An apple a day keeps the doctor away" came from the Old English saying "To eat an apple before bed will make the doctor beg his bread." —101 Foods

KANSAS PUDDING

PREP TIME:
5 MINUTES

BAKE:
35 MINUTES

OVEN: *350°*

1 cup apples, peeled, minced
½ cup walnuts, chopped
1 egg, well beaten
1 tsp. baking powder
½ tsp. kosher salt
⅛ tsp. cinnamon
1 tsp. vanilla
¾ cup sugar
3 T (rounded) flour

MAKES 4 SERVINGS

Mix all ingredients and bake in a greased 1 quart baking dish. Bake at 350° for 35 minutes.

TIP: *I am not sure of the origin of Kansas Pudding. It is much like a bread pudding or a stuffing. Good with breakfast, but it also makes a great side dish served with pork or as a dessert served with vanilla ice cream.*

An apple a day keeps the doctor away.

PREP TIME: 15 MINUTES   CHILL: 30 MINUTES

- ¼ cup raisins
- 2 T fresh orange juice
- 1 tsp. vanilla
- 4 oz. cream cheese, softened
- ¼ cup sour cream
- 2 T sugar
- zest of 1 orange, finely grated
- 2 cups fresh fruit, sliced or cut up
- ½ cup low-fat granola

MORNING PARFAIT

MAKES 4 SERVINGS

In a small micro-safe bowl, combine raisins and orange juice. Cover and microwave on high for 30 to 45 seconds; let stand 1 minute to plump raisins. Stir in vanilla; set aside.

In a medium bowl, whisk together cream cheese, sour cream, and sugar until smooth. Stir in the raisin mixture and orange zest. Chill for about 30 minutes.

In 4 parfait glasses, layer half the cream cheese mixture, half the fruit and then half the granola. Repeat the layers.

TIP: *About any combination of fruit will work but I recommend strawberries, blueberries, raspberries, and peaches. Drizzle top with a little honey or top with additional orange zest for a garnish if desired.*

PREP TIME: 5 MINUTES   CHILL: OVERNIGHT

- ½ cup sour cream
- 2 T sugar
- 1 T fresh orange juice
- ½ tsp. orange zest, finely grated
- 4 bananas
- 4 T granola

HEAVENLY BANANAS

MAKES 4 SERVINGS

Mix together sour cream, sugar, orange juice, and orange zest. Cover tightly and refrigerate overnight. Slice 1 banana in each serving dish. Stir the sour cream mixture well. Top each banana with 2 tablespoons. Sprinkle granola on top and serve immediately.

GRAPEFRUIT MERINGUE PUDDING PIE

1 large grapefruit, halved
1 T cornstarch
⅓ cup + 2 T sugar, divided
dash of salt
¼ cup water
1 T lemon juice
1 tsp. butter
dash hot pepper sauce
1 egg, separated
⅛ tsp. cream of tartar
1 to 2 T shredded coconut

MAKES 2 SERVINGS

Juice grapefruit; strain and reserve ¾ cup of juice. Pull out the membrane from shells; cover and reserve shells in refrigerator. Mix together cornstarch, ⅓ cup sugar, and salt in a medium saucepan. Add grapefruit juice and water. Bring mixture to boil, stirring constantly until smooth and thick. Stir in lemon juice and butter. Lightly beat hot pepper sauce into egg yolk. Remove grapefruit sauce from heat; stir in egg yolk mixture. Return to heat; cook and stir 2 minutes; remove from heat and cool to touch. Evenly divide mixture into the 2 reserved grapefruit shells.

Beat egg white with cream of tartar until foamy. Add remaining sugar; beating until stiff and glossy. Spoon the meringue on top of grapefruit filling, sealing at edges. Sprinkle coconut over top of each grapefruit. Place in baking pan; bake at 425° for 8 to 10 minutes or until golden. Cool in refrigerator for 1 hour or until completely chilled before serving.

PREP TIME:  COOK:
30 MINUTES   *30 MINUTES*

6 whole Bartlett pears
1 cup port wine
½ cup light brown sugar
1 tsp. cinnamon
juice and zest of one lemon
½ cup raspberry jam
frozen whipped topping,
  thawed

POACHED PEARS

MAKES 6 SERVINGS

Peel and core pears; set aside. Mix the port wine, brown sugar, cinnamon, lemon juice, and zest in a large sauce pan. Bring to a boil and cook over moderate heat for 10 minutes. Add the pears to the wine sauce (liquid should cover the pears) and poach for 15 to 20 minutes. Remove the pears from the sauce; set aside. Continue to cook the sauce to reduce by half. Add raspberry jam and continue to cook, stirring constantly until jam is dissolved and well blended. Place pears into serving dishes, pour the sauce over pears and top with whipped topping.

HOW TO RIPEN PEARS QUICKLY

Place pears in a paper bag and store it in a dark, cool, and ventilated place. The paper bag traps the ethylene gas produced by pears which helps to soften more quickly.

To speed up the ripening even more, add an apple, banana, or avocado to the bag. Ripe pears can be stored in the refrigerator for about 3 to 5 days. ——Wisegeek.com

Pears for breakfast!

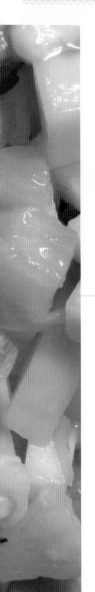

LEMONY SWEET FRUIT SALAD

PREP TIME:
10 MINUTES

CHILL:
10 MINUTES

2 T fresh lemon juice
2 T honey
1 tsp. Dijon mustard
¼ tsp. kosher salt
⅛ tsp. black pepper
2 T canola oil
3 cups cantaloupe, seeded, cubed
4 cups pineapple, cored, cubed
1 cup blueberries
2 cups nectarines (4 medium), peeled, sliced

MAKES 8 SERVINGS

In a small bowl, whisk together lemon juice, honey, Dijon mustard, salt, and pepper until blended. Add oil in a slow steady stream, whisking constantly, until dressing is thick and emulsified.

Combine fruit in a large bowl. Chill for 10 minutes or until ready to serve. Just before serving toss fruit with dressing.

TIP: *This salad is also delicious with strawberries, blackberries, honeydew, and watermelon. You can also use lime or orange juice as a substitute for the lemon.*

HITTING THE JUICE
Oranges, lemons, or grapefruit that are heavy for their size and have smoother, thinner skins tend to yield more juice.

CHAPTER FOUR

KEEPING IT LIGHT
MAIN-DISH SALADS & SIDE SALADS

SMOKEY TORTELLINI SALAD
DUCK CONFIT SALAD
HEARTY SALAD BOWL
THANKSGIVING SALAD
SEVEN LAYER SALAD
TURNER SALAD LE MONT
HOT CHICKEN SALAD
 CASSEROLE
BAKED SEAFOOD SALAD
CRAB SALAD
SHRIMP SALAD
LOBSTER & EGG LAMAZE
SALMON PEAR SALAD
SWEET & SOUR WILTED SALAD
BLACK EYED PEAS, BACON
 'N SPINACH

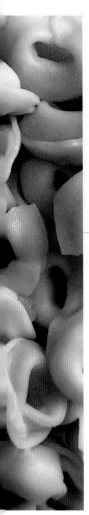

SMOKEY TORTELLINI SALAD

½ cup mayonnaise
¼ cup milk
½ tsp. dried whole oregano
½ tsp. garlic powder
¼ tsp. black pepper
1 15 oz. can light kidney beans, drained, rinsed
½ lb. smoked sausage, diced
2 green onions, thinly sliced
8 oz. cheese tortellini, cooked, drained
Parmesan cheese, grated (optional)

MAKES 6 SERVINGS

Combine mayonnaise, milk, oregano, garlic powder, and pepper in a medium saucepan over medium heat; stir until blended. Add beans, sausage, and onions; continue to cook, stirring occasionally, until heated thoroughly, about 10 minutes.

Stir tortellini into the sauce; simmer for 5 minutes or until heated through. Add parmesan cheese to top of salad if desired; serve immediately or refrigerate and serve cold.

TIP: *Tortellini is navel shaped pasta typically filled with cheese, meat or a leafy green like spinach.*

PREP TIME: CHILL:
15 MINUTES   *1 HOUR*

2 T walnut oil
2 T Balsamic vinegar
juice of 1 lemon
kosher salt & black pepper
   to taste
1 12 oz. pkg. duck confit
3 endives, thinly sliced
   crosswise
1 cup walnuts, toasted
½ cup dried cherries or
   currants
1 cup Roquefort, crumbled

DUCK CONFIT SALAD

MAKES 4-6 SERVINGS

Whisk together oil, vinegar, lemon juice, salt, and pepper; set aside. Heat duck confit and remove from bone. Roughly chop duck, walnuts, and cherries. Combine endive, duck, walnuts, cherries, and vinaigrette; cover and refrigerate for 1 hour. Just before serving add Roquefort; toss lightly.

TIP: *Substitute gorgonzola cheese for a slightly milder taste. If you cannot find duck confit in your grocery store, you can easily make it. See the recipe below.*

EASY DUCK CONFIT
Wash and pat dry ¾ lb. duck legs and thighs. Prick skin all over with knife or needle being careful to not pierce the meat. Salt the legs very well and let rest at room temperature for 20 minutes. Lightly oil a baking dish just big enough to hold the legs then place legs in dish skin side up.
Bake legs at 300° for 1½ hours or until the skin is starting to look crispy and is partially submerged in fat. Increase oven to 375° and continue to cook for 15 minutes or until skin is light golden brown. Remove and let cool 10 to 15 minutes.

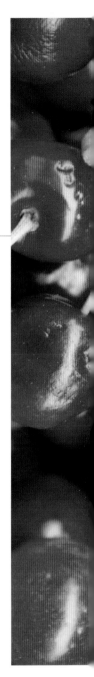

HEARTY SALAD BOWL

1 cup French style green beans
1 cup carrot, sticks, cooked
1 cup celery, sticks
½ cup French dressing
1 head lettuce cut in wedges
1 cup beef or ham, cooked, cut into ¼" strips
½ cup Swiss cheese, cut into ¼" strips
2 eggs, hard boiled, sliced
¾ cup mayonnaise
2 T horseradish
¼ cup chili sauce

MAKES 6-8 SERVINGS

Mix green beans, carrots, and celery together. Cover with French dressing and place in refrigerator for 2 hours. Drain excess dressing from vegetables; set aside. Arrange lettuce wedges around a salad bowl. Place the meat, cheese, and marinated vegetables in center of lettuce wedges. Arrange eggs in a circle on top in center. Combine mayonnaise, horseradish, and chili sauce; beat until well blended. Pour over meat and vegetables arrangement just before serving.

THANKSGIVING SALAD

½ pint whipping cream
½ cup Miracle Whip salad dressing
4 cups shredded cabbage
1 20 oz. can pineapple, drained
1 large apple, diced
1 cup green grapes, halved
1 cup small marshmallows
1 banana, sliced

MAKES 8 SERVINGS

Whip the whipping cream until stiff. Combine all ingredients except the banana. Cover and chill for about 1 hour. Fold in banana just before serving.

PREP TIME: CHILL:
20 MINUTES   *OVERNIGHT*

1 head iceberg lettuce,
  shredded

½ cup Roma tomatoes,
  seeds removed, chopped

½ cup green pepper, diced

¼ cup almonds, sliced,
  toasted

¼ cup green onions, sliced

½ cup celery, diced

1 10 oz. pkg. frozen peas

½ lb. bacon, cooked,
  crumbled

1¼ cups mayonnaise

2 T sugar

⅔ cup Parmesan cheese,
  grated

1 cup cheddar cheese,
  shredded

SEVEN LAYER SALAD

MAKES 12 SERVINGS

In a glass serving dish, layer the first 8 ingredients. Whisk together mayonnaise, sugar, and parmesan; spread on top of salad. Cover dish and refrigerate overnight or for at least 8 hours. Top with cheeses just before serving.

BACON MADE EASY

For a no hassle, no splatter, and easy clean-up way to cook bacon line a baking sheet with aluminum foil, lay bacon strips out on a shallow baking pan in a single layer. Bake at 350° for about 20 minutes; flip bacon strips and cook for another 5 minutes or until crisp. Drain bacon on paper towels. When the baking sheet cools, carefully fold up foil with bacon drippings and discard.

Did somebody say *bacon?*

TURNER SALAD LE MONT

MAKES 6 SERVINGS

Dressing:
- 1 large egg + 1 large egg yolk
- ½ cup sugar
- ½ tsp. dry mustard
- 1½ tsp. cornstarch
- ¼ cup water
- ¼ cup distilled white vinegar
- ¼ tsp. kosher salt
- 2 T unsalted butter, cubed, softened
- ½ cup mayonnaise

Salad:
- 4 cups broccoli flowerets, blanched
- 1 cup raisins
- 1 cup mushrooms, sliced
- ½ cup red onion, chopped
- 6 slices bacon, cooked, crumbled
- kosher salt & black pepper to taste

In a small sauce pan, combine water, vinegar, and salt; bring to a boil over medium heat. In a small bowl, whisk together egg, egg yolk, sugar, mustard, and cornstarch. Add the egg mixture to boiling water and vinegar and cook for 1 minute whisking continuously or until thickened. Remove the pan from heat; whisk in the butter then mayonnaise. Cover and chill the dressing for at least 1 hour.

In a large bowl, gently combine the broccoli, raisins, mushrooms, onion, and bacon. Just before serving, pour dressing over salad and toss well. Season salad with salt and pepper to taste.

Healthy and delicious.

PREP TIME: BAKE:
20 MINUTES   *30 MINUTES*

OVEN: *350°*

4 cups chicken breast, cooked, cubed (about 1⅓ lb.)

1½ cups brown or white rice, cooked

1 10¾ oz. can cream of chicken soup

¼ cup chicken broth

¼ cup onion, chopped

¼ cup green pepper, chopped

¼ cup celery, chopped

¾ cup mayonnaise

4 eggs, hard boiled

1 cup sharp cheddar cheese, shredded

½ cup potato chips, crushed

Hot Chicken Salad Casserole

MAKES 6 SERVINGS

Combine chicken, rice, soup, broth, onion, green pepper, celery, and mayonnaise. Slice hard boiled eggs and carefully fold into mixture. Pour into lightly greased 2 quart casserole dish. Top with grated cheese and crushed potato chips. Bake for 30 minutes.

TIP: *1 pound of boneless, skinless chicken breast equals approximately 3 cups of cubed chicken. Dress up this dish by adding slivered almonds to the top. You can also reduce the eggs to 2 or 3.*

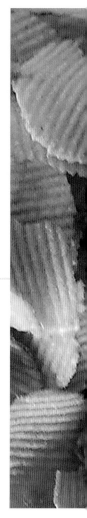

BAKED SEAFOOD SALAD

1 4½ oz. can tiny shrimp, drained, rinsed
1 6½ oz. can crabmeat
½ cup green pepper, diced
¼ cup onion, minced
1 cup celery, diced
⅔ cup mayonnaise
1 tsp. Worcestershire sauce
½ tsp. kosher salt
¼ tsp. black pepper
½ cup dry bread crumbs
1 T butter, melted

MAKES 4 SERVINGS

Cut shrimp in half lengthwise and combine with crabmeat, green pepper, onion, and celery. In a separate bowl, mix mayonnaise, Worcestershire sauce, salt, and pepper. Stir into seafood mixture. Pour into lightly greased 1 quart casserole dish. Toss the breadcrumbs with melted butter and sprinkle over top. Bake uncovered, at 350° for 40 minutes. Serve on greens or with bread or crackers.

TIP: *This recipe is better using fresh shrimp, cooked and roughly chopped, in lieu of canned. Spice it up with 1 to 2 minced jalapeño peppers or a dash of Tabasco sauce. Also, try substituting cream of potato soup for the mayonnaise.*

CRAB SALAD

- 1 6.4 oz. pkg. Rice-A-Roni, prepared
- 8 oz. crabmeat, cooked, rinsed, flaked
- ½ cup celery, thinly sliced
- ¼ cup green onions, thinly sliced
- 1 8 oz. container sour cream or yogurt
- lemon wedges

MAKES 4 SERVINGS

Combine rice with crabmeat, celery, and onions. Add sour cream into rice mixture; blend thoroughly. Cover and refrigerate for 1 hour or until chilled. Serve with lemon wedges.

SHRIMP SALAD

PREP TIME:
10 MINUTES

CHILL:
1 HOUR

- 1 6.4 oz. box chicken flavored rice mix, prepared
- 1 6 oz. jar marinated artichoke hearts
- ½ cup green bell pepper, diced
- 4 green onions, thinly sliced
- 1 4 oz. can tiny shrimp, rinsed, drained
- ⅓ cup mayonnaise

MAKES 6-8 SERVINGS

Drain artichokes, reserving juice and coarsely chop. Combine rice mix, artichokes, green pepper, onions, and shrimp. Combine the reserved juice with mayonnaise. Add to rice mixture; mixing well. Cover and chill salad for 1 hour before serving.

LOBSTER & EGG LAMAZE

MAKES 6 SERVINGS

- 1 10¾ oz. can condensed tomato soup
- 1 cup mayonnaise
- ¼ cup sweet pickle relish
- ½ tsp. onion powder
- ½ T Dijon mustard
- 1 T fresh lemon juice
- 2 cups lobster (3 medium tails), roughly chopped
- 4 cups lettuce, torn in pieces
- ¼ cup green pepper, diced
- ½ cup celery, diced
- 3 hardboiled eggs, diced

Dressing: In a medium size bowl, blend soup with the mayonnaise. Add relish, onion powder, mustard, and lemon juice. Mix well and chill in refrigerator for 1 hour.

Salad: Divide lettuce between plates. Toss lobster with green pepper and celery. Add mixture on top of lettuce. Top with eggs.

At serving time, pour enough dressing over salad and lightly toss to coat. Serve remaining dressing on the side.

TIP: *Imitation lobster or crab, also known as paddock, can be substituted if fresh lobster is unavailable if you're looking for a cheaper alternative.*

Sweet and savoury!

PREP TIME: CHILL:
15 MINUTES   *1 HOUR*

⅓ cup extra virgin olive oil
3 T white wine vinegar
1 oz. blue cheese, crumbled
1 tsp. sugar
¼ tsp. black pepper
⅛ tsp. kosher salt
1 pear halved, peeled, thinly
   sliced
1 6 oz. can pink salmon,
   drained, picked through,
   flaked
1 rib celery, thinly sliced
3 T pecans, chopped
fresh spinach leaves
   (optional)

SALMON PEAR SALAD

MAKES 4 SERVINGS

In a small bowl, whisk together oil, vinegar, cheese, sugar, pepper, and salt. Cover and refrigerate until serving time. Spoon 3 tablespoons of vinaigrette over pear slices, tossing to coat thoroughly. Combine salmon, celery, pecans, and 3 tablespoons of vinaigrette; toss gently to coat.

To serve, line individual salad plates with spinach, arrange pear slices over spinach leaves and top with salmon mixture. Add additional vinaigrette if desired.

SWEET & SOUR WILTED SALAD

4 cups Romaine lettuce, torn in pieces
1 11 oz. can mandarin oranges, drained
1 16 oz. can cut green beans, drained
1 16 oz. can sliced carrots, drained
½ cup orange juice, divided
1 T corn starch
½ cup apple cider vinegar
2 T sugar
¾ tsp. Chinese hot chili oil
1 lb. shrimp, peeled, deveined

MAKES 4 SERVINGS

Line the bottom of a clear glass bowl with ¼ of lettuce. Arrange oranges over lettuce; top with additional ¼ lettuce, green beans, ¼ lettuce, carrots and remaining lettuce; set aside.

Combine ¼ cup orange juice with cornstarch; set aside. Combine remaining orange juice, vinegar, sugar, and oil in a medium saucepan over medium-high heat. Bring to a boil, stirring constantly, until sugar is dissolved. Reduce heat; add corn starch mixture and cook, stirring constantly until thickened.

Add shrimp and continue to cook for 3 minutes or until shrimp is pink or not translucent and sauce is slightly thickened. Arrange shrimp on top of lettuce, pour glaze on top and serve immediately.

PREP TIME: COOK:
20 MINUTES   20 MINUTES

- 2 16 oz. cans black eyed peas, drained
- 5 T extra virgin olive oil, divided
- 6 slices bacon, crisp, crumbled
- 5 T red wine vinegar, divided
- ½ tsp. Tabasco hot pepper sauce
- ½ tsp. ground cinnamon
- 1 clove garlic, minced
- 2 tsp. Heinz 57 sauce
- 1 6 oz. bag fresh baby spinach leaves
- 2 oz. fresh mushrooms, thinly sliced

BLACK EYED PEAS, BACON 'N SPINACH

MAKES 6 SERVINGS

Heat 1 tablespoon olive oil in a medium saucepan. Add black eyed peas, 1 tablespoon vinegar, hot sauce, cinnamon, and garlic over medium-high heat. Bring to boil, reduce heat and simmer for 10 minutes.

Combine remaining olive oil, bacon, remaining vinegar, and steak sauce in a small saucepan over medium-high heat until heated thoroughly, about 5 minutes. Add sauce into pea mixture and combine well.

To serve, place peas on a bed of spinach leaves and garnish with mushrooms.

TOPPING IT OFF
SAUCES & DRESSINGS

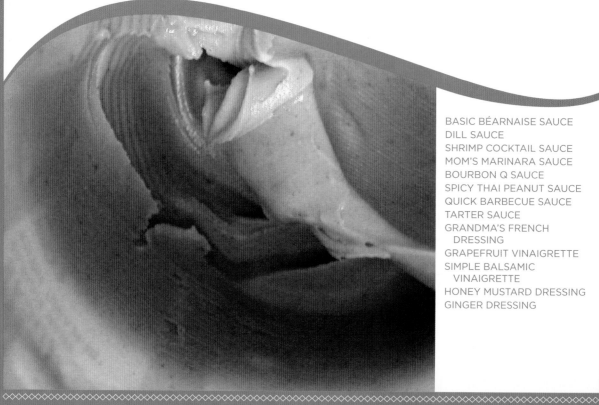

PREP TIME:
10 MINUTES

1 T shallots, minced
1 T fresh tarragon, chopped
1 T fresh parsley, chopped
½ cup white vinegar
3 egg yolks, well beaten
2 T cold water
½ cup butter or margarine,
   cut into small pieces
kosher salt & black pepper
   to taste

BASIC BÉARNAISE SAUCE

MAKES ½ CUP

Place shallots, tarragon, parsley, and vinegar in a small saucepan. Boil quickly to reduce to half. Add egg yolks and water; reduce heat to low.

Gradually add butter piece by piece into sauce (you may not use all the butter), whisking continually until sauce is thickened. Season sauce with salt and pepper and keep warm to serve with meat.

HOLLANDAISE & BÉARNAISE SAUCES

Both sauces are essentially warm flavored mayonnaises. They have lots of butter that is emulsified with egg yolks into a small amount of acidified liquid.

Hollandaise sauce ingredients include water, lemon juice, salt, pepper, egg yolks, and butter. It is traditionally served with poached fish, boiled or steamed vegetables, and with Eggs Benedict.

Béarnaise sauce substitutes vinegar for the water and lemon, and you may add shallots, tarragon, chervil, parsley, thyme, bay leaf, or cayenne pepper. It is most often served with grilled meat or fish. ——ochef.com

DILL SAUCE

½ cup plain fat-free yogurt
or sour cream
2 T green onions, minced
½ tsp. fresh dill, minced
¼ tsp. garlic, minced

MAKES ½ CUP

Mix all ingredients and refrigerate for at least 2 hours to allow flavors to infuse.

SHRIMP COCKTAIL SAUCE

PREP TIME:
5 MINUTES

CHILL:
1 HOUR

½ cup chili sauce
⅓ cup ketchup
2 to 3 T horseradish sauce
1½ tsp. Worcestershire
sauce
¼ tsp. salt
2 T fresh lemon juice
dash of pepper
dash of Tabasco sauce

MAKES 1 CUP

Mix all ingredients. Chill in the refrigerator for 1 hour before serving.

Mouth-watering.

PREP TIME:  COOK:
1 HOUR   *4-6 HOURS*

- 1½ lb. sweet Italian pork sausage, bulk
- 1½ lb. beef, cubed small
- 4 cups onion (3 medium), minced
- 4 cups green pepper, minced
- 8 cloves garlic, minced
- 2 28 oz. cans whole tomatoes, broken-up
- 2 28 oz. cans crushed tomatoes
- 2 28 oz. cans tomato sauce
- 2 6 oz. cans tomato paste, divided
- 2 4.25 oz. cans black olives, diced
- 8 oz. fresh mushrooms, diced small
- 1 to 2 T sugar, or to taste
- ¼ cup fresh parsley or 1 T dried
- 1 T fresh oregano or 1 tsp. dried
- 1 tsp. salt or to taste
- ½ tsp. black pepper or to taste

MOM'S MARINARA SAUCE

MAKES 12-16 SERVINGS

In a large stock pot, brown the beef and sausage, breaking into bits, drain if necessary; set aside. In the same pan, sauté the onions and green pepper, scrapping and cleaning the residual meat (fond) from pan, until onion is soft and translucent. Add garlic and cook 1 minute.

Add beef and sausage into the onion and pepper mixture. Add whole tomatoes, crushed tomatoes, tomato sauce, and 1 can of tomato paste. Cook over medium heat, stirring occasionally, until heated through. Add in black olives, mushrooms, and seasonings. Reduce heat to low and continue to simmer for 4 to 6 hours stirring occasionally. Add the remaining can of tomato paste to thicken if necessary 15 minutes before serving.

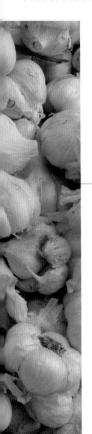

BOURBON Q SAUCE

PREP TIME: 10 MINUTES

COOK: 30 MINUTES

SET: *1-2 DAYS*

2 cups ketchup
¼ cup tomato paste
¾ cup bourbon
⅓ cup apple cider vinegar
¼ cup Worcestershire sauce
½ cup brown sugar, packed
⅓ tsp. hot pepper sauce
½ onion, minced
4 garlic cloves, minced
½ tsp. black pepper
½ T kosher salt

MAKES 2½ CUPS

In a large skillet combine onion, garlic, and bourbon. Bring to a simmer over medium-low heat and cook for 10 minutes or until onion is translucent. Be careful to keep bourbon away from flame or from getting hot too fast. Add remaining ingredients, bring to a boil, then reduce heat to low and simmer for 20 minutes.
Strain sauce and refrigerate uncovered, for 1 to 2 hours. Seal in an airtight container and store in refrigerator for 1 to 2 days to allow flavors to meld together.

WARNING!
Heating alcohol to a boil may result in a loss of flavor, and in extreme cases, cause a flash fire. Alcohol is less dense and will evaporate at a lower temperature than water. It is best to warm alcohol slowly.

TIP: *Use Crystal, Franks Original or Louisiana hot pepper sauce.*

SPICY THAI PEANUT SAUCE

PREP TIME: 5 MINUTES

CHILL: 1 HOUR

⅓ cup water
⅔ cup peanut butter
⅓ cup soy sauce
2 T fresh lemon juice
1 T cayenne pepper
¼ cup light corn syrup
¼ cup dry sherry

MAKES 2 CUPS

Add all ingredients into a blender or food processor. Blend sauce on low for 1 minute or until well blended. Spoon over chicken, seafood, or Asian lettuce wraps.

TIP: *This sauce does have a spicy kick. Reduce or eliminate the cayenne for a milder sauce.*

PREP TIME:
5 MINUTES

COOK:
15 MINUTES

2 cups ketchup
½ cup molasses
⅓ cup bourbon
⅓ cup Dijon mustard
2 T Worcestershire sauce
2 T Crystal or Franks hot pepper sauce
2 tsp. onion powder
1 tsp. garlic salt
¼ cup light brown sugar, packed
¼ tsp. Liquid Smoke

QUICK BARBECUE SAUCE

MAKES 2½ CUPS

Combine all ingredients in a medium saucepan. Bring mixture to a simmer over medium heat; stirring constantly. Lower heat to medium–low and simmer uncovered, for about 15 minutes, stirring occasionally, until thickened.

SAUCY HISTORY

How did all those amazing flavors get packed into a bottle of Worcestershire sauce? The story begins in the early 1800s, in Worcester, England. An English nobleman returned home from his travels in India eager to replicate a sauce recipe he had tasted. He enlisted two chemists, John Lea and William Perrins to, through trial and error, make up a batch of the sauce.

The initial results were not impressive. They found the taste unpalatable and set the jars in their cellar to gather dust. A few years later, they stumbled across them and decided to taste the contents again. To their delight, the aging process had turned it into a delicious, savory sauce. Although there are numerous homemade Worcestershire sauce recipes, the original recipe, now owned by the H. J. Heinz Company, is still a closely guarded secret. —leaperrins.com

TARTAR SAUCE

1 cup mayonnaise
1 tsp. onion, grated
1 T capers, chopped
1½ T sweet pickle relish
1 T pimiento-stuffed olives, chopped
dash cayenne pepper

MAKES 1½ CUPS

Combine all ingredients; stir until well blended. Chill for at least 1 hour before serving.

GRANDMA'S FRENCH DRESSING

1 10¾ oz. can condensed tomato soup
1½ cups corn oil
¾ cup vinegar
¾ cup sugar
1½ tsp. kosher salt
1 tsp. paprika
1 tsp. dry mustard
1 tsp. celery seed
dash of black pepper
2 tsp. Worcestershire sauce
2 tsp. onion, grated
1 clove garlic, crushed

MAKES 4½ CUPS

Combine all ingredients in a blender until smooth. Chill 1 hour before serving. Dressing can be stored in refrigerator for up to 2 weeks.

PREP TIME:
5 MINUTES

¼ cup fresh grapefruit juice
¼ cup walnut oil
2 tsp. Dijon mustard
1 tsp. garlic, minced
kosher salt & black pepper
   to taste

GRAPEFRUIT VINAIGRETTE

MAKES ½ CUP

Place all ingredients into a jar, cover and shake well. Refrigerate until needed.

PREP TIME:
5 MINUTES

¼ cup balsamic vinegar
2 tsp. dark brown sugar
   (optional)
1 T garlic, minced
½ tsp. kosher salt
½ tsp. freshly ground black
   pepper
¾ cup olive oil

SIMPLE BALSAMIC VINAIGRETTE

MAKES 1 CUP

Whisk together vinegar, sugar, garlic, salt, and pepper until the sugar and salt dissolves. Beat in the olive oil by droplets, whisking constantly. Taste and adjust seasoning if necessary.

HONEY MUSTARD DRESSING

5 T medium body honey
3 T smooth Dijon mustard
2 T rice wine vinegar

MAKES ½ CUP

Combine all ingredients in a bowl and whisk until smooth. Serve as a dressing over greens, drizzled over steamed vegetables, or as a dip for meat.

GINGER DRESSING

½ cup canola oil
2½ T gingerroot, peeled, minced
¼ cup onion, chopped
¼ cup sesame seed, toasted
½ teaspoon ketchup
½ tsp. sugar
⅛ tsp. celery seed
1 pinch ground black pepper
1½ T soy sauce
⅓ cup rice wine vinegar

MAKES 1 CUP

Combine all ingredients except soy sauce and vinegar in a blender or food processor. Blend ingredients on high for 1 minute or until creamy. Add soy sauce and vinegar; whisk or blend on low for another 30 seconds.

CHAPTER SIX

LET'S GET COOKING!
SOUPS, STEWS, & CHILIS

CANNELLINI & CABBAGE SOUP
EDAMAME SOUP & FETA
  CROUTONS
TORTELLINI SOUP
ITALIAN STEWED TOMATOES
SHERRY CORN CHOWDER
HOPPIN' JOHN BLACK EYED
  PEAS
BIG BATCH JAMBALAYA
BRUNSWICK STEW
SOUPER TOMATO BEEF STEW
VENISON STEW & BISCUITS
CHICKPEA STEW OVER
  COUSCOUS
RATATOUILLE
CHILI VERDE
WHITE CHICKEN CHILI

1 T olive oil
3 cups cabbage, thinly sliced
2 carrots, thinly sliced in coins
6 garlic cloves, minced
1 tsp. dried thyme
¼ tsp. black pepper
2 14 oz. cans chicken broth
1 14.5 oz. can diced tomatoes, un-drained
1 cup water
¼ cup tomato paste
2 15 oz. cans cannellini beans, drained, rinsed

MAKES 6 SERVINGS

Heat olive oil in a large stock pot over medium-high heat. Cook cabbage, carrots, garlic, thyme, and pepper for 2 to 3 minutes. Stir in broth, tomatoes, water, and tomato paste. Bring to a boil, reduce heat, and simmer, covered, for 8 to 10 minutes or until vegetables are tender, stirring occasionally.

Mash half of the beans then add all of the beans to the vegetables mixture. Heat through and serve.

TIP: *Make this delicious soup a little heartier by adding ½ lb. of cooked ham or chicken and top with shredded Parmesan cheese. Delicious!*

¾ cup sweet onion, chopped

4 tsp. canola oil, divided

2 medium carrots, thinly sliced into coins

2 garlic cloves, minced

2 14 oz. cans chicken or vegetable broth

1 12 oz. pkg. frozen edamame

1½ tsp. fresh thyme, roughly chopped

1 egg white

1 T water

½ cup panko bread crumbs

4 oz. feta cheese, cut into ¾" cubes

fresh thyme leaves (optional)

EDAMAME SOUP & FETA CROUTONS

MAKES 4 SERVINGS

In a large saucepan, cook onion in 2 teaspoons of oil over medium heat for 5 minutes. Add carrots and garlic; cook and stir 1 minute more. Add broth, edamame, and thyme. Bring to a boil; reduce heat and simmer uncovered, for 10 minutes or until the carrots and edamame are tender.

Meanwhile, whisk together water and egg white in a small bowl until frothy. Place bread crumbs in another small bowl. Dip feta cheese into egg white mixture then coat with bread crumbs.

In a skillet, heat remaining oil over medium-high heat. Add feta; cook 2 to 3 minutes or until browned but not softened, turning carefully to brown on all sides. Ladle soup into bowls, top with feta croutons and fresh thyme if desired.

TIP: *Edamame is also known as young soy beans.*

TORTELLINI SOUP

PREP TIME:  COOK:
5 HOUR   15 MINUTES

1 10 oz. pkg. frozen
  chopped spinach
2 14.5 oz. cans fat-free
  chicken broth
2 14.5 oz. cans Italian
  stewed tomatoes
1 15 oz. jar Italian sauce
1 9 oz. pkg. fresh tortellini
  pasta

MAKES 4-6 SERVINGS

In a 5 quart pan, combine the spinach, chicken broth, stewed tomatoes, and Italian sauce. Bring to a boil while breaking up the spinach and tomatoes. Add tortellini and simmer 7 minutes.

TIP: *You can substitute diced tomatoes if you want a smoother or less chunky consistency. If you don't have or cannot find the Italian blend on the store shelf, below is a "from scratch" recipe:*

ITALIAN STEWED TOMATOES

PREP TIME: COOK:
1 HOUR   50 MINUTES

24 large tomatoes,
  peeled, seeded, chopped
1 cup celery, chopped
½ cup onion, chopped
¼ cup green pepper,
  chopped
2 tsp. dried basil
1 T sugar

MAKES 12 PINTS

Combine all ingredients in a 5 quart pan. Cover and cook for 10 minutes, stirring occasionally. Pour in mason jars, seal, and boil in hot water bath for 40 minutes.

PREP TIME: COOK:
5 MINUTES   *15 MINUTES*

1 T vegetable oil
½ cup onion, diced
⅓ cup green pepper, diced
1 14.5 oz. can whole kernel
   corn, drained
1 14.5 oz. can cream style
   corn
1½ cups chicken broth
¾ cup heavy cream
¼ cup dry sherry
dash ground nutmeg
kosher salt & black pepper
   to taste

SHERRY CORN CHOWDER

MAKES 4-6 SERVINGS

In a 3 quart saucepan, heat oil over medium-high heat. Add onion and green pepper; cook 5 minutes or until soft, stirring frequently. Add whole corn, cream corn, chicken broth, cream, sherry, nutmeg, salt, and pepper. Bring to boil, reduce heat to medium-low, cover and cook for 5 minutes.

WHY YOU SHOULD EAT CORN

Corn, a time-honored food staple for 7000 years, is a good source of fiber, vitamin B1, folate, vitamin C, and pantothenic acid. Corn is also loaded with heart health and cancer-fighting properties.

Besides being nutritious, corn products can be helpful to keep around the house. Cornmeal boiled with milk can be applied to burns, inflammations, and swellings. More than just a thickener, apply cornstarch as a powder to soothe chaffed skin or diaper rash.
——101 foods

HOPPIN' JOHN BLACK EYED PEAS

1 lb. dried black eyed peas, soaked

2 small ham hocks or meaty ham bones

2 medium onions, divided

1 bay leaf

3 large garlic cloves, halved

1 cup long-grain white rice

1 10 oz. can Rotel tomatoes with chilies, un-drained

1 medium red bell pepper, chopped

½ green bell pepper, chopped

3 ribs celery, chopped

1 jalapeño pepper, minced

2 tsp. Cajun or Creole seasoning

½ tsp. dried thyme leaves

¾ tsp. ground cumin

¾ tsp. kosher salt

4 green onions, thinly sliced (optional)

MAKES 10 SERVINGS

In a large Dutch oven or kettle, combine peas, ham, and 6 cups of water. Cut 1 onion in half and add it to the pot along with bay leaf and garlic. Bring to a boil then reduce heat to medium-low and simmer gently for 2 to 2½ hours or until beans are tender but not mushy. Remove ham, cut meat from the bone, dice and set aside. Drain peas, discarding onion, bay leaf, and garlic; set aside.

Add 2½ cups water to the pot; bring to boil. Add rice, cover and simmer 10 to 12 minutes. Mince the remaining onion and add to the rice along with the peas, tomatoes and their juices, red and green bell peppers, celery, jalapeño pepper, and seasonings. Cook 5 to 8 minutes or until rice is tender. Stir in green onions and ham. Serve with hot sauce and corn bread.

PREP TIME: *45 MINUTES* **COOK:** *45 MINUTES*

- 1 boneless skinless chicken breast, cooked, cubed
- 2 T olive oil, divided
- ½ lb. fully cooked ham, cubed
- ½ lb. smoked kielbasa sausage, cubed
- 2 green peppers, roughly chopped
- 2 medium onions, roughly chopped
- 6 medium garlic cloves, minced
- 2 14.5 oz. cans beef broth
- 1 28 oz. can crushed tomatoes
- 1½ cups water
- ¾ cup Dijon mustard
- 2 T Worcestershire sauce
- ¼ cup fresh parsley, minced
- 1½ tsp. cayenne pepper
- ½ tsp. dried thyme
- 1½ cups long grain rice, raw
- 1 lb. shrimp, peeled, deveined
- 6 green onions, diced

BIG BATCH JAMBALAYA

MAKES 10-12 SERVINGS

Heat oil in a Dutch oven or stock pot. Cook the ham, sausage, peppers, and onions until onions are tender. Add garlic and cook 1 minute longer.

Stir in broth, tomatoes, water, mustard, Worcestershire, parsley, cayenne, and thyme. Bring to a boil, reduce heat, cover and simmer for 10 minutes.

Add rice and return to a boil. Reduce heat, cover and simmer another 25 to 30 minutes or until rice is tender. Stir in shrimp and chicken and cook additional 2 to 4 minutes or until the shrimp turns pink.

Garnish with green onions.

BRUNSWICK STEW

YIELDS 4 QUARTS

Stew: Melt butter in a 2 gallon stock pot. Add potatoes, onions, chicken broth, chicken, and pork. Bring to boil, stirring occasionally, until potatoes are near done. Add peas, tomatoes, beans, corn, Liquid Smoke and sauce. Slow simmer, stirring occasionally, for 2 hours.

Sauce: Melt butter in a large saucepan. Add ketchup, mustard, and vinegar, blending until smooth. Add garlic, black and red pepper, Liquid Smoke, Worcestershire, hot sauce, and lemon juice. Blend until smooth and add dark brown sugar. Simmer for 10 minutes.

Stew:
1 cup butter
3 cups potatoes, diced
1 cup onion, diced
2 14.5 oz. cans chicken broth
1 lb. chicken, white & dark, cooked, diced
1 7.5 oz. pkg. smoked pork chops, diced
1 8.5 oz. can early peas, drained
2 14.5 oz. cans stewed tomatoes, broken-up
1 16 oz. can baby lima beans, drained
1 14.5 oz. can creamed corn
¼ cup Liquid Smoke

Sauce:
¼ cup butter
1¾ cup ketchup
¼ cup French's yellow mustard
¼ cup white vinegar
½ T garlic, chopped
1 tsp. coarse black pepper
½ tsp. crushed red pepper
1 T Liquid Smoke
2 T Worcestershire sauce
2 T Crystal pepper hot sauce
½ T fresh lemon juice
¼ cup dark brown sugar

PREP TIME:
10 MINUTES

COOK:
*2 HOURS,
20 MINUTES*

¼ cup flour
½ tsp. kosher salt
¼ tsp. black pepper
1 lb. beef, cubed
2 T olive oil
1 10¾ oz. can condensed
  tomato soup
1¼ cup water (1 can)
12 pearl onions, peeled
1 cup frozen peas
3 Yukon gold potatoes,
  quartered
¼ tsp. dried thyme

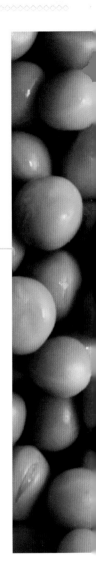

SOUPER TOMATO BEEF STEW

MAKES 6 SERVINGS

Coat beef in flour, salt, and pepper. In a large Dutch oven, brown cubed beef in oil. Add tomato soup and water. Cover and simmer for 1½ hours; stirring occasionally. Add onions, peas, potatoes, and thyme. Cover and simmer for another 45 minutes or until done.

HOW TO EASILY PEEL PEARL ONIONS
• *Fill a pot with water and bring to a boil.*
• *Cut off the tip of each onion opposite the root end.*
• *Boil onions in the pot for 2 minutes then drain.*
• *Drop onions into a bowl of ice water, allow to cool, remove, and drain.*
• *Squeeze the root end and the onion will pop out.*
• *Cut off the remaining roots.*

Scrumptious!

VENISON STEW & BISCUITS

PREP TIME: 20 MINUTES   COOK: 2½-3 HOURS

4 lbs. venison, cut into ½" cubes
1 medium onion, chopped
2 T of vegetable oil
1 T garlic, minced
2 4 oz. cans mushrooms stems & pieces
1 28 oz. can of whole tomatoes, un-drained
2 6 oz. cans of tomato paste
2 cups hot water
2 T sugar
1 tsp. kosher salt
½ tsp. ground black pepper
2 bay leaves
2 tsp. dried thyme
2 tsp. dried marjoram
1 tsp. dried oregano
4 cups carrots, sliced in coins
corn meal to thicken

Biscuits:
4 cups Bisquick
1 cup butter melted
16 oz. container of sour cream

MAKES 8 SERVINGS

Cook venison, onions, and garlic in oil in a Dutch oven until meat is brown. Add mushrooms, tomatoes, tomato paste, water, sugar, and seasonings. Heat to boiling, reduce heat; cover and simmer for 1½ hours, stirring occasionally or until meat is almost tender. Add carrots; cover and simmer for 30 minutes.

Gradually add corn meal as necessary to thicken. Heat stew to a boil, stirring constantly; boil 1 minute. Reduce heat to simmer.

Biscuits: Mix all ingredients until a soft dough forms (about 20 strokes). Pour venison stew into a 9" x 13" baking dish. Drop dough mixture by spoonful's on top of venison. Bake stew at 450° for 20 minutes or until biscuits are brown.

PREP TIME:
10 MINUTES

COOK:
3-5 HOURS

1 lb. dried chickpeas
1 medium onion, chopped
2 tsp. dried oregano, divided
4 cups water
1 lb. zucchini, cut into ¾" pieces
1 14.5 oz. can diced Italian tomatoes
½ cup vegetable broth
1 tsp. kosher salt
½ tsp. black pepper
whole wheat couscous, prepared
1 cup feta cheese, crumbled

CHICKPEA STEW OVER COUSCOUS

MAKES 8 SERVINGS

Soak chickpeas overnight. Drain, rinse and place chickpeas into a slow cooker with onion and 1 teaspoon of oregano; add water. Cook for 3 hours on High or 5 hours on Low or until peas are tender. Drain chickpea mixture and return to slow cooker. Stir in zucchini, tomatoes, and broth; cover and cook for another 2 hours. Stir in remaining oregano, salt, and pepper just before serving. Serve stew over couscous and sprinkle with feta cheese.

POTLUCK

Back in the Middle Ages, people would throw all of their leftover food into a pot of water that was kept boiling most of the time. This makeshift stew was eaten by the family or fed to strangers when there was no other food to offer. Since the food was thrown in the pot at random, its quality or taste depended entirely on luck.

RATATOUILLE

MAKES 8 SERVINGS

PREP TIME: COOK:
30 MINUTES   *1½ HOURS*
OVEN: *350°*

Heat oil in a large stock pot; add onions and cook until softened. Bundle herbs together and add into pot along with tomatoes, eggplant, and peppers. Simmer covered, on top of stove or bake in oven at 350° for 45 minutes. Add in the zucchini and cook an additional 35 to 45 minutes. Remove herbs and drain off juices; boil down to syrupy liquid.

TIP: *Serve over rice, top with chopped basil or parsley and serve hot or cold. If served cold, toss with a little olive oil just before serving.*

½ cup extra virgin olive oil
1 lb. onions, finely sliced
1 14.5 oz. can whole tomatoes, un-drained
1 lb. eggplant, cut into 1" cubes
1 lb. red & green peppers, cubed
2 garlic cloves, crushed, lightly salted
8 coriander seeds, crushed
3 parsley sprigs
1 bay leaf
1 sprig of marjoram
1 sprig of thyme
kosher salt & black pepper to taste
1 lb. zucchini, cut 1" thick slices
¼ cup fresh basil or parsley, chopped

Tomatoes, eggplant, and peppers, oh my!

PREP TIME:
20 MINUTES

COOK:
3 HOURS

2½ lbs. pork chops, ½" thick
2 cups onion, chopped
3 garlic cloves, crushed
1 14 oz. can chicken broth
1 T coriander seed, crushed
1 tsp. kosher salt
1 tsp. ground black pepper
1 bay leaf
1 30 oz. can crushed
   tomatillos
1 30 oz. can diced green
   chilies
⅓ cup fresh cilantro,
   chopped

CHILI VERDE

MAKES 8 SERVINGS

De-bone and de-fat pork chops, reserving the bones. Cut meat into ½ inch cubes. Brown the meat in a stew pot adding onions halfway through browning. Add garlic just before finishing the browning. Cover with chicken broth adding water if necessary. Heat to a boil, cover and simmer for about 2½ hours or until the meat is tender.

Brown the bones, cover with water and add bay leaf. Simmer for 3 hours, adding water if necessary. Remove and discard bones and bay leaf. Strain and set stock aside.

Meanwhile, soak the crushed coriander seed in hot water for about 30 minutes. Drain seeds and add to pork mixture along with salt and pepper.

When the meat is tender, add reserved stock, tomatillos, green chilies, and cilantro. Adjust the salt if needed.

TIP: *For more heat, add 1 tablespoon diced jalapeño with the onion.*

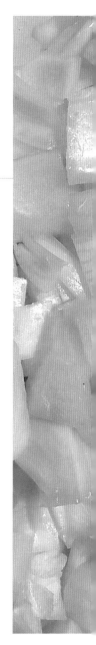

WHITE CHICKEN CHILI

3 T olive oil, divided
2 lbs. boneless chicken breast, cubed
2 cups onion, chopped
2 garlic cloves, minced
2 tsp. cumin
1 tsp. ground coriander
½ tsp. dried oregano
1 8 oz. can green chilies, chopped
1 cup water
2 15.5 oz. cans cannelloni beans, drained, rinsed
1 14 oz. can chicken broth
½ tsp. hot pepper sauce
1 cup Monterey Jack cheese, shredded (optional)

MAKES 6-8 SERVINGS

Heat 2 tablespoons of olive oil in a large pot over medium-high heat. Add chicken and cook for 10 minutes or until brown, stirring frequently. Remove chicken from pot; set aside.

In same pot, heat remaining oil and sauté onion for 6 minutes. Add garlic; sauté for 2 minutes, stirring frequently. Stir in cumin, coriander, and oregano; continue to cook 1 minute.

Stir in chilies, chicken, water, cannelloni beans, and broth; reduce heat to low and cook partially covered, for 20 minutes. Add in hot sauce. Ladle chili into each bowl and top with cheese if desired.

CHAPTER SEVEN

ON A SIDE NOTE
GREAT ACCOMPANIMENTS

BROCCOLI CASSEROLE

PREP TIME: 5 MINUTES   COOK: *18-20 MINUTES*

OVEN: *350°* BAKE: *30 MINUTES*

¼ cup onion, diced
6 T butter, divided
2 T flour
½ cup water
1 8 oz. jar pasteurized cheese
2 10 oz. pkgs. frozen chopped broccoli, thawed
3 eggs, well beaten
12 soda crackers, crushed

MAKES 6-8 SERVINGS

Sauté onion in 4 tablespoons of butter for 8 minutes or until softened; stir in flour. Reduce heat to low and slowly add water, stirring constantly, until mixture thickens and comes to a boil. Add cheese; continue to cook until cheese melts and is well blended.

Drain broccoli well and chop small if necessary. Add to cheese sauce. Add eggs, mixing gently until blended. Turn mixture into a greased 1½ quart casserole dish. Cover with crushed soda cracker crumbs. Dot the top with remaining butter. Bake at 350° for 30 minutes.

EAT YOUR BROCCOLI

Broccoli is loaded with vitamins, minerals, sulfur compounds and is rich in powerful cancer fighting phytonutrient antioxidants. It supports heart, digestive, vision, bone health, and promotes a healthy pregnancy due to high folic acid and B–vitamins essential in proper cell division and DNA synthesis.

The best way to tap into the nutrients is to cut broccoli into small pieces and let rest for 5 minutes before cooking. Steaming broccoli is the best way to retain nutrients but cook only until al dentè *(soft outside, crisp inside.) Overcooking causes as much as a 50% loss in nutrients.* ——The World's Healthiest Foods

PREP TIME: 20 MINUTES      COOK: 15-20 MINUTES

1 1½ lbs. head cauliflower
kosher salt to taste
¼ cup milk
2 T unsalted butter
1 T fresh lemon juice
2 T fresh parsley, chopped
fresh ground pepper to
    taste

CAULIFLOWER IN PARSLEY BUTTER SAUCE

MAKES 4 SERVINGS

Break cauliflower into large flowerets. Place the cauliflower in a pot, add cold water to cover. Bring to a boil, add milk and salt to taste; simmer for 12 to 15 minutes. Do not overcook. Drain well. Melt butter in a large sauté pan. Add lemon, parsley, pepper, and flowerets; gently toss to coat.

PREP TIME: 20 MINUTES   COOK: 30 MINUTES
OVEN: 350°

1 head cauliflower, cut into
    flowerets
1 6 oz. tub chive & onion
    cream cheese

CHEESY CAULIFLOWER

MAKES 6 SERVINGS

Steam cauliflower then partially mash in a bowl. Add cream cheese; mix well. Put mixture into a small baking dish and bake at 350° for 30 minutes.

CREOLE STYLE GREEN BEANS

PREP TIME: *20 MINUTES*   COOK: *20 MINUTES*

- 6 slices bacon, diced
- ¾ cup onion, diced
- ½ cup green pepper, diced
- 2 T flour
- 2 T brown sugar, packed
- 1 T Worcestershire sauce
- ½ tsp. kosher salt
- ¼ tsp. freshly ground black pepper
- ⅛ tsp. dry ground mustard
- 1 14.5 oz. can whole tomatoes
- 1 16 oz. can whole green beans, drained

MAKES 6 SERVINGS

Cook bacon until crisp, remove from skillet, reserving 3 tablespoons of drippings; set bacon bits aside. Add onion and green pepper to bacon drippings; cook until tender.

Blend in flour, brown sugar, Worcestershire sauce, salt, pepper, and mustard. Add in tomatoes, breaking up into pieces. Continue to cook, stirring constantly, until thickened. Add beans; heat through. Top with bacon bits.

CREOLE & CAJUN STYLES

The cooking styles of the Louisiana Creoles and Cajuns are very close. Both cultures are immigrants of France and Spain. The primary difference in cuisine evolved more from culture or class than the ingredients in the cuisine. Many Creoles were rich planters who aspired to eat fine cuisine and relied heavily on hired chefs. The Cajuns were tough, frugal people who lived off the land.

There is an old saying that may sum it up: "A Creole feeds one family with three chickens, a Cajun feeds three families with one chicken."——Gumbopages.com

PREP TIME: COOK:
5 MINUTES   5 MINUTES
CHILL: *OVERNIGHT*

2 14.5 oz. cans cut green
  beans, drained
1 medium red bell pepper,
  julienned
1 small onion, thinly sliced,
  separated
1 cup sugar
¾ cup cider vinegar
1 tsp. celery seeds

PICKLED GREEN BEANS

MAKES 10 SERVINGS

Combine green beans, red pepper, and onion in a medium bowl; set aside.

In a small saucepan, combine sugar, vinegar, and celery seeds. Cook on medium-high heat for 5 minutes or until the mixture is boiling and sugar is dissolved.

Combine sugar and green bean mixtures in an airtight container. Cover and refrigerate overnight. Serve cold.

TIP: *Jazz it up by adding 2 to 3 julienned Serrano or jalapeño peppers. This is a perfect side dish with a Mexican fiesta or summer barbecue.*

Sweet!

Sour!

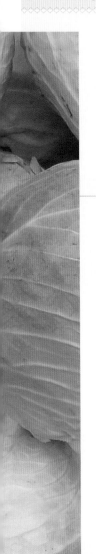

FREEZER COLESLAW

1 medium head cabbage, shredded
1 tsp. kosher salt
2 cups sugar
1 cup cider vinegar
¼ cup water
1 tsp. celery seed
1 tsp. mustard seed
1 large carrot, shredded
½ cup green pepper, diced

MAKES 10 SERVINGS

In a large bowl, combine cabbage and salt; let stand for 1 hour. Meanwhile, in a large saucepan, combine sugar, vinegar, water, celery seed, and mustard seed. Bring to a boil; boil 1 minute; remove from heat to cool. Add vinegar mixture, carrot, and green pepper to cabbage. Chill before serving or transfer to freezer storage bags; seal and freeze up to 2 months. Remove from freezer 2 hours before serving.

THE FRESHER THE BETTER

It is best to always use fresh cabbage and not pre-shredded in a bag. Shredded cabbage begins to slowly lose nutritional value soon after being cut. Select a cabbage head that is dense, firm, bright in color and only a few outer leaves are loose.

Fresh cabbage is very low in fat and calories and is loaded with vitamins, minerals, and cancer preventing phyto-chemicals. Because cabbage is prone to insects, conventional farming often uses insecticides. It's best to rinse cabbage under running water, then soak the cabbage in saline water for 30 minutes, and rinse again in clean water.

PREP TIME: 20 MINUTES   COOK: 10 MINUTES
BROIL: 5 MINUTES

- 3 T butter
- ½ tsp. kosher salt
- ½ tsp. dry ground mustard
- ⅛ tsp. paprika
- 3 T flour
- ½ cup milk
- ½ tsp. Worcestershire sauce
- ½ cup cheddar cheese, grated
- 1 10 oz. pkg. frozen chopped spinach, cooked
- 4 eggs, cooked and sliced

SPINACH & EGG CASSEROLE

MAKES 4 SERVINGS

Melt butter in a saucepan, then add salt, dry mustard, paprika, and flour; stir to a paste. Add in milk gradually, stirring constantly until thickened. Add Worcestershire sauce, remove from heat and let stand for about 5 minutes. Add cheddar cheese, stirring until well combined.

Put spinach in the bottom of a greased 1 quart casserole dish. Arrange egg slices on top of spinach and cover with cheese sauce. Cook 4 to 5 inches below broiler for 5 minutes or until brown.

PREP TIME: 20 MINUTES   SLOW COOK: 2 HOURS
OVEN: 350°

- 2 16 oz. cans baked beans
- ¼ cup light brown sugar, packed
- ½ tsp. dry ground mustard
- ½ cup ketchup
- 1 cup onions, chopped
- 1 tsp. Worcestershire sauce

BASIC BAKED BEANS

MAKES 8 SERVINGS

Combine all ingredients in a slow cooker. Cover and cook on high for 2 hours.

SKILLET WHITE BEANS

MAKES 10-12 SERVINGS

PREP TIME: COOK:
20 MINUTES   30 MINUTES

1 medium onion, halved, thinly sliced
3 T butter
½ cup maple syrup
⅓ cup white balsamic vinegar
2 T light brown sugar, packed
2 T fresh sage, roughly chopped
2 T tomato paste
1 tsp. kosher salt
½ tsp. freshly ground black pepper
2 16 oz. cans navy beans, drained, rinsed
2 16 oz. cans butter beans, drained, rinsed
1 16 oz. can garbanzo beans, drained, rinsed

In a 12 inch skillet, cook onion in melted butter over medium heat for about 15 minutes. Stir in maple syrup, vinegar, brown sugar, sage, tomato paste, salt, and pepper. Add beans; stir to coat. Cover and continue to cook for 10 to 15 minutes, stirring occasionally.

MINUTE RICE BARBECUE

MAKES 4 SERVINGS

PREP TIME: COOK: 5-15
20 MINUTES   MINUTES

1⅓ cup water
½ tsp. kosher salt
2 T butter
2 T onion, minced
1 tsp. prepared mustard
2 T chili sauce
1 tsp. Worcestershire sauce
¼ tsp. pepper
1⅓ cups Minute Rice (4⅝ oz. pkg.)

Outdoor Instructions: Line a bowl with a double layer of foil. Combine all ingredients in bowl. Lift the foil from the bowl creating a packet; seal ends of packet. Place the foil packet over hot coals or grill for 15 minutes. Open and stir with fork.

Indoor Instructions: Combine water and all ingredients except rice in large saucepan or skillet; bring to a boil. Add rice and mix just to moisten the rice. Cover and remove from heat. Let stand 5 minutes. Toss lightly with fork.

PREP TIME:  COOK:
10 MINUTES   *15 MINUTES*

3 cups frozen lima beans,
  cooked
6 thick slices bacon, cut
  into ½" pieces
1 medium onion, chopped
6 to 8 fresh mushrooms,
  halved, sliced
⅔ cup sour cream
1 tsp. curry powder
Seasoning salt to taste
hot sauce to taste
  (optional)

LIMA BEANS

MAKES 8 SERVINGS

Cook bacon pieces in a large skillet until crisp. Drain bacon grease reserving 2 tablespoons. Sauté onions and mushrooms in reserved grease over medium heat until onions are translucent. Add bacon, sour cream, curry, and seasoning salt; mixing well. Taste and adjust seasonings if necessary.

Remove skillet from heat and add in lima beans; mixing well. Serve immediately or keep warm.

SPILLING THE BEANS

Named after the capital of Peru, lima beans are a great high-fiber, low fat source of protein and minerals, are low in sugar, and have no cholesterol.

Also called butter or chad beans, lima beans are starchy but buttery in texture. One popular American lima bean dish is Succotash.

Lima beans are high in molybdenum which helps detoxify the sulfites found in many food and beverage preservatives.

Many western countries, including the US restrict the growing of lima beans because lima beans contain a cyanide compound. Only varieties with low cyanide levels are allowed.

ANDOUILLE STUFFED MUSHROOMS

PREP TIME: COOK:
20 MINUTES   5 MINUTES
OVEN: *375°* BAKE: *10 MINUTES*

2 8 oz. pkgs. button
  mushrooms
2½ T vegetable oil, divided
2 Andouille sausage links
1 5 oz. pkg. Boursin
  cheese
½ tsp. paprika
¼ tsp. kosher salt
¼ tsp. black pepper

MAKES 2-3 DOZEN

Trim the stems from the mushrooms and discard. Cut a thin slice from the top of each mushroom so that it will set level when turned upside down. Heat ½ tablespoon of oil in a sauté pan. Add the thin mushroom slices and cook 2 minutes or until softened; set aside.

Add remaining oil to pan and sauté the mushroom caps for 2 minutes each side. Drain on a paper towel and let cool completely. Peel and chop sausage then place in a food processor or blender with cheese, paprika, pepper, salt, and mushroom slices. Blend well. Place mushroom caps on a baking sheet. Roll the sausage mixture into balls and place into mushroom caps. Bake at 375° for 5 minutes, until heated through.

TIP: *When buying fresh mushrooms, look for caps that are closed around the stem. Avoid mushrooms that show the black or brown gills.*

Slice and sauté!

BRAISED MUSHROOMS

PREP TIME:
10 MINUTES

COOK:
20 MINUTES

- 2 T unsalted butter
- 1 medium shallot, diced
- 3 large fresh sage leaves, diced
- 1 cup red wine
- ¼ tsp. kosher salt
- ¼ tsp. black pepper
- 1 lb. mushrooms, halved

MAKES 4 SERVINGS

Melt butter in a 10 inch skillet over medium heat. Add shallot and sage; cook for 2 minutes. Add wine, salt, and pepper; boil on high for 1 minute. Stir in mushrooms, reduce heat to medium, cover; cook for 5 minutes. Uncover; continue to cook for 12 minutes or until tender, stirring occasionally.

FOOD OF THE GODS

Not generally thought of as nutrition packed vegetables, mushrooms are loaded with more selenium (brain food) than any other produce and are a good source of vitamin D. Mushrooms have been used medicinally for thousands of years to ward off cancers, fight heart disease, migraines, and build a strong immune system.

Ancient Egyptians believed that mushrooms were endowed with special powers that granted eternal life. Since only Pharaohs would be worthy of this gift, common people were not allowed to touch a mushroom, let alone eat one. Similarly, ancient Romans believed that the god Jupiter created mushrooms by casting lightning bolts to the ground during thunderstorms. They referred to mushrooms as the "Food of The Gods." —101 foods, The World's Healthiest Foods

4 CHEESE POTATO STUFFED MUSHROOMS

PREP TIME: *20 MINUTES* COOK: *2 MINUTES*

OVEN: *450°* BAKE: *10 MINUTES*

- 1 lb. large fresh whole mushrooms
- 2 T unsalted butter or olive oil
- 1 24 oz. bag Ore-Ida Steam n' Mash potatoes
- 2 cups Mexican 4 shredded cheese
- 3 T chives, chopped, divided
- ¾ tsp. kosher salt

MAKES 2 DOZEN

Remove stems from mushrooms and discard. Carefully scoop out mushroom caps. Cut a thin slice from the top of each mushroom so that it will set level when turned upside down; discard slices.

Sauté the mushroom caps in butter or oil for 2 minutes on each side. Remove from heat, drain on a paper towel until cool enough to handle.

Prepare the potatoes per package directions. Add cheese, 2 tablespoons chives, and salt. Fill each mushroom with potato mixture, mounding it slightly. Bake at 450° for 10 minutes or until potato stuffing is golden brown. Top with remaining chives.

PICKLED MUSHROOMS

PREP TIME:
10 MINUTES

COOK:
5 MINUTES

CHILL: *4-6 HOURS*

- ⅔ cup tarragon vinegar
- ½ cup vegetable oil
- 2 T water
- 1 T sugar
- 1½ tsp. kosher salt or to taste
- 1 clove garlic, minced
- 1 dash Tabasco hot pepper sauce
- 1 lb. mushrooms, cleaned
- 1 medium red onion, thinly sliced
- 1 red pepper, thinly sliced

MAKES 4 SERVINGS

In a small saucepan, whisk together vinegar, oil, water, sugar, salt, garlic, and hot sauce over medium-high heat until sugar is dissolved. Remove from heat, cool and pour into an airtight container. Add mushrooms, onion, and pepper into oil mixture and toss.

Marinate in refrigerator 4 to 6 hours to allow the flavors to infuse into mushrooms. Mushrooms will keep in refrigerator for 1 week. You can also put marinated mushrooms in canning jars filling to ½ inch from top and process in a boiling water bath for 20 minutes. Canned mushrooms should keep about 2 months.

TIP: *Select bright, small to medium mushrooms with unopened caps that have short stems. I prefer to break or twist stems off. Also, I recommend draining before serving.*

Delectable!

COLCANNON

MAKES 4-6 SERVINGS

4 large potatoes, quartered, peeled, boiled
¼ cup butter, softened
¼ cup milk
2 T olive oil
2 cups cabbage, shredded
1 cup onion, chopped
kosher salt & black pepper to taste

Coarsely mash potatoes with butter and milk; set aside. In a large skillet, heat oil over medium-high heat. Sauté cabbage and onions until vegetables are limp, about 7 to 10 minutes. Combine mashed potatoes with the vegetable mixture; stir until heated through. Season colcannon with salt and pepper to taste.

THE SKILLET POT

"Did you ever eat Colcannon, made from pickled cream? With the greens and scallions mingled like a picture in a dream. Did you ever make a hole on top to hold the melting flake of the creamy, flavored butter that your mother used to make?"
The Chorus:
"Yes you did, so you did, so did he, so did I. And the more I think about it sure nearer I am to cry. Oh, wasn't it the happy days when troubles we had not, and our mothers made Colcannon in the little skillet pot." —Wikipedia

PREP TIME: 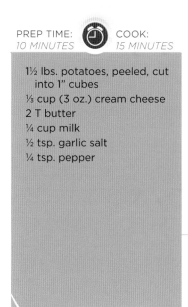 COOK:
10 MINUTES   *15 MINUTES*

- 1½ lbs. potatoes, peeled, cut into 1" cubes
- ⅓ cup (3 oz.) cream cheese
- 2 T butter
- ¼ cup milk
- ½ tsp. garlic salt
- ¼ tsp. pepper

EASY WHIPPED POTATOES

MAKES 4 SERVINGS

In a large pot, cover potatoes in water and bring to a boil. Lightly salt water and cook potatoes for 15 minutes or until tender. Drain. Combine potatoes with remaining ingredients and beat on medium-high with mixer until smooth.

ONE POTATO, TWO POTATO

Choosing the right potatoes to mash is a personal preference. Some prefer a creamy smooth mashed potato while others like it chunky or just smashed. Here are a few tips that may help you select the right potato to get your desired result:
• Russet: high starch, low water, baking, frying, decent to mash, absorbent, good with butter.
• Yukon Gold: medium starch, high water, all-purpose, holds up to boiling, works for most potato dishes, do not over mix.
• Red: less starch, waxy, holds shape, good for soups, stews, salads and scalloped, good mashed.
—Thekitchn.comabout.com

ULTIMATE MASHED POTATOES

3½ cups chicken stock
5 large potatoes, peeled, 1" cubed
½ cup light cream
½ cup sour cream
¼ cup fresh chive
2 T butter
3 slices bacon, cooked, crumbled
1 generous dash of black pepper

MAKES 6 SERVINGS

Heat the broth and potatoes in a 3 quart saucepan over medium-high heat. Bring to a boil; reduce heat to medium and cook covered, for about 10 minutes or until potatoes are tender. Drain potatoes, reserving broth. Mash potatoes with ¼ cup of reserved broth and remaining ingredients, adding more reserved broth if needed to get desired consistency.

ONION SOUP POTATOES

8 russet potatoes, scrubbed
½ cup butter (1 stick), melted
1 2 oz. pkg. onion soup mix

MAKES 8 SERVINGS

Slice potatoes crosswise into thin slices, keep the potato intact. Place each potato on a sheet of aluminum foil. Sprinkle onion soup mix over top and drizzle with melted butter. Wrap foil tightly around potatoes and place on a shallow baking pan. Bake in 375° oven for 35 to 45 minutes.

TIP: *This is a great recipe for a camp-out. You can add other vegetables and meat to make it a stew. Place each wrapped "stew" in the indirect heat around the campfire and cook for 35 to 45 minutes or until desired doneness.*

PREP TIME: 10 MINUTES   BAKE: 40-50 MINUTES

OVEN: 400°

2 T olive oil
6 medium Yukon gold
  potatoes
½ tsp. dried oregano
½ tsp. dried chives
½ tsp. dried parsley
1 T garlic, roasted, minced
kosher salt & black pepper
  to taste

OVEN ROASTED YUKONS

MAKES 4 SERVINGS

Lightly grease a 9" x 13" baking dish with oil. Coarsely chop potatoes into 2 inch chunks and place in baking dish. Sprinkle potatoes with herbs and garlic. Bake potatoes uncovered, at 400° for 40 to 50 minutes, stirring occasionally until the potatoes are lightly browned and crispy.

ROASTING GARLIC

Roasting garlic makes it easier to handle, it's 2 to 4 times milder than raw garlic and it adds an enhanced smoky or roasted flavor to the dish. It may sound daunting to roast garlic but it's really simple to do. Just follow these four easy steps:

1. Cut ½ inch off the top off the garlic bulb.
2. Place the bulb with cut side up in a custard cup or other oven safe dish and drizzle with olive oil.
3. Cover with foil and bake at 400° for 25 minutes.
4. Cool and gently squeeze the base of the bulb to push out the roasted cloves.

Crispy!

POTATO CAULIFLOWER GRATIN

1 small head cauliflower, cored, quartered, sliced

1½ lbs. Yukon gold potatoes, peeled, sliced

3 cups whole milk

¼ cup water

2 T cornstarch

¼ tsp. nutmeg, freshly grated

½ cup Gruyere cheese, shredded, divided

kosher salt & black pepper to taste

MAKES 8 SERVINGS

Heat a large covered pot of water to a boil. Add cauliflower and boil for 3 minutes or until tender; drain and set aside.

Meanwhile, in a large skillet, heat potatoes and milk on medium-high heat just until boiling, stirring occasionally. Reduce heat and simmer 7 to 10 minutes. Dissolve cornstarch with water and stir into potato mixture; simmer for 3 minutes or until thickened. Add cauliflower, nutmeg, ¼ cup cheese and season with salt and pepper.

Transfer half of the potato mixture into a greased 3 quart baking dish. Top with remaining cheese. Spread the remaining potato mixture evenly over cheese. Bake at 350° for 30 to 35 minutes or until tender when pierced with a knife. Let stand 15 minutes before serving.

PREP TIME: BAKE:
20 MINUTES *40 MINUTES*

OVEN: *400°*

- 3 lbs. potatoes, peeled, cut into 1½" cubed
- ½ cup olive oil
- 4 garlic cloves, minced
- 1½ tsp. dried oregano, crumbled
- 1 tsp. kosher salt
- freshly ground black pepper to taste
- ½ cup beef or chicken stock
- ⅓ cup fresh lemon juice
- 2 to 3 T fresh oregano garnish (optional)

LEMON & GARLIC ROASTED POTATOES

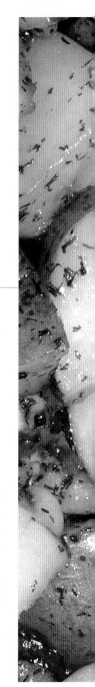

MAKES 8 SERVINGS

Preheat oven to 400°. Place potatoes in a single layer in a 9" x 13" baking dish and drizzle oil over top. Add the garlic, dried oregano, salt, and pepper; toss to coat. Bake for 15 minutes, add stock, toss to coat and bake for 10 minutes. Add the lemon juice; bake 10 to 15 minutes or until the potatoes are cooked through.

MINCING WORDS

The more garlic is minced, sliced or pressed the more pungent smelling and stronger tasting it is. But the good news is it's also healthier. Garlic contains numerous health promoting nutrients that are released by the process of the mincing. Here is my easy way to mince garlic:

1. Break a clove from the head. Loosen the skin, by placing the flat side of a chef's knife on the clove and give it a whack with the butt end of your hand.

2. Slice garlic horizontally, then slice vertically keeping clove intact. Rotate and chop through the clove.

3. Let garlic sit for 5 to 10 minutes before cooking.

LOADED POTATO SKINS

PREP TIME:
20 MINUTES

BROIL:
7 MINUTES

10 slices bacon, cooked, crumbled
5 large russet potatoes, baked
2 T olive oil
½ tsp. kosher salt
¼ tsp. fresh ground black pepper
2½ cups cheddar cheese, shredded
3 green onions, thinly sliced
½ cup sour cream

MAKES 5 SERVINGS

Slice potatoes in half lengthwise. Scoop out flesh leaving about ¼ inch edge (discard flesh or reserve for another use). Place skins, cut-side down and brush lightly with oil.

Position the oven rack 6 inches below broiler. Broil 4 minutes. Remove skins from oven. Flip over, season skins with salt and pepper.

Sprinkle each skin with 1 to 2 tablespoons of cheese; add crumbled bacon and another 1 to 2 tablespoons of cheese.

Return to broiler; broil 3 minutes until cheese melts. Top with green onions and a dollop of sour cream.

NOT ONLY SKIN DEEP

There is a popular belief that all the nutrition is held within the skin of the potato. Not true, more than fifty percent of the nutrition is within the flesh of the potato. So don't sell yourself short; eat the whole thing. —101 foods

PREP TIME:  BAKE:
10 MINUTES   *50 MINUTES*

OVEN: *450°*

2 large sweet potatoes, peeled, cut into 1" cubes

2 medium sweet onions, cut into 1" cubes

3 T olive oil

¼ cup amaretto liqueur or maple syrup

1 tsp. dried thyme

kosher salt & fresh ground pepper to taste

¼ cup almonds, toasted

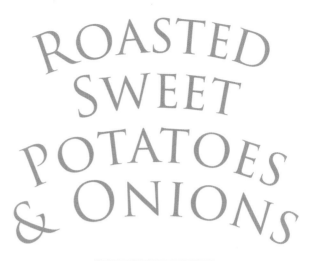

ROASTED SWEET POTATOES & ONIONS

MAKES 6 SERVINGS

Place sweet potatoes into a medium baking dish. Combine oil, amaretto or syrup, thyme, salt, and pepper. Toss potatoes and onions with the oil mixture. Bake in 450° oven, covered, for 30 minutes. Uncover; bake an additional 20 minutes. Sprinkle top with almonds.

I YAM WHAT I YAM

Did you know sweet potatoes aren't really potatoes at all? Potatoes come from the Solanaceae *family while the sweet potato comes from the* Convolvulaceae *family. They are not Yams either. A "Yam," derived from the African word* nyami, *is a huge root vegetable from Africa that is starchier and less sweet than a sweet potato.*

But enough with the big words; sweet potatoes may be one of the oldest vegetables known to humans, dating back 10,000 years and is still today considered to be one of the most nutritious. They have about twice the dietary fiber than russet potatoes and are loaded with vitamins C and A. —The world's healthiest foods, 101 foods

SWEET POTATO FRIES

PREP TIME:
5 MINUTES

BROIL:
10 MINUTES

1 T sugar
1 tsp. kosher salt
1 tsp. ground cumin
1 tsp. ground dark chili powder
2 medium sweet potatoes, scrubbed
1 to 2 T olive oil

MAKES 4 SERVINGS

In a small bowl, combine sugar, salt, cumin, and chili powder; set aside. Cut the sweet potato crosswise into ¼ inch thick slices and place on a lightly greased baking sheet.

Brush slices with olive oil and sprinkle with half the seasoning mixture; broil for 5 minutes. Turn slices over, brush with oil, sprinkle with seasonings and broil an additional 5 minutes.

TIP: *I make up this mix of seasonings in large batches to keep on hand. It works great as a seasoning or rub on a variety of vegetables, chicken, pork, salmon, and shrimp.*

CHAPTER EIGHT

GOOD OLE CHUCK
GROUND MEAT DISHES

WHATS YOUR BEEF?

GROUND BEEF (73% LEAN, 27% FAT)—High in fat but is tender, flavorful and juicy. The meat comes from the underbelly and breast of the cow and fat is adding in when ground. It's great for burgers and meatloaf but due to the high fat content, it loses a lot of its size during cooking.

GROUND CHUCK (80% LEAN, 20% FAT)—This meat is from the shoulder and neck area. A little chewy but the marbling is already in the meat leaving a flavorful and juicy burger or meatloaf.

GROUND ROUND (85% LEAN, 15% FAT)—Comes from the rear or rump of the cow. High in flavor but is a tad tougher to chew. Good for tacos, Sloppy Joes, Hamburger Helper and slow cooker meals.

GROUND SIRLOIN (90% LEAN, 10% FAT)—Leaner and better for those watching their weight or the very health conscious. Sirloin does not bind well so it is best suited for cooking lasagna, pasta dishes, and chili.

BAKED BEANS & MEATBALLS

PREP TIME:
10 MINUTES
COOK:
10 MINUTES

OVEN: *350°* BAKE: *40 MINUTES*

1 lb. ground beef
2 15 oz. cans baked beans
2 T fresh parsley, chopped
¼ cup ketchup
1 tsp. kosher salt
¼ cup sweet pickle relish
⅛ tsp. black pepper
2 T light brown sugar
1 T vegetable oil
¼ tsp. chili powder
¼ cup onion, diced

MAKES 4-6 SERVINGS

Combine ground beef, parsley, salt, and pepper. Shape into about 16 small meatballs. In a large skillet, brown meatballs and onions in oil; cook until onion is tender. Combine beans, ketchup, relish, sugar, and chili powder in a 2 quart casserole. Stir in about 10 meatballs and onions. Scatter remaining meatballs on top. Bake in 350° oven for 40 minutes.

THE BEST CANNED BAKED BEANS

With so many brands of canned baked beans to choose from, which one is the best choice? This may help you make your decision a little easier. With the help of my husband, who fancies himself somewhat of a "baked bean connoisseur," we blind taste tested the 4 brands commonly found on most grocery shelves. And the winner was….

Heinz Premium Vegetarian Beans in Rich Tomato Sauce won hands down. Rich in both taste and texture, it stands on its own as a side course or is a great choice to use as a base for a baked bean dish.

PREP TIME: COOK:
10 MINUTES *10 MINUTES*
OVEN: *350°* BAKE: *30 MINUTES*

- 1 lb. ground beef
- ⅓ cup fine dry bread crumbs
- 2 T onion, minced
- 1 tsp. kosher salt
- 1 egg, slightly beaten
- 1 10¾ oz. can tomato soup, divided
- 2 T vegetable oil
- 1 tsp. chili powder
- ¼ cup water

CHILI MEATBALLS

MAKES 4 SERVINGS

Combine ground beef with bread crumbs, onion, salt, egg, and about ¼ of the can of soup. Shape into 1 inch meatballs. Heat vegetable oil in a large skillet and brown meatballs.

Mix remaining soup, chili powder and water together. Put meatballs in a 1 quart casserole. Pour soup mixture over meatballs. Cover and bake at 350° for about 30 minutes.

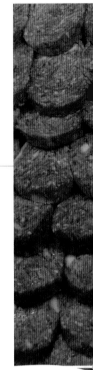

PREP TIME:  BROIL:
5 MINUTES *10 MINUTES*

- 1 lb. ground beef
- 1 12 oz. jar beef gravy, divided
- ¼ cup dry bread crumbs
- 2 T onion, minced
- 1 tsp. kosher salt
- ¼ tsp. freshly ground black pepper
- 1 4 oz. can mushrooms, drained

STEAK BURGER

MAKES 4 SERVINGS

Combine ground beef with ½ cup of the gravy (⅓ of jar), bread crumbs, onion, salt, and pepper. Broil 5 minutes on each side. Add mushrooms to the remaining gravy, heat and pour over steak.

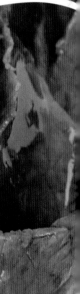

PREP TIME: BAKE:
10 MINUTES   1 HOUR
OVEN: *350°*   SET: *10 MINUTES*

1 lb. ground beef
⅓ cup evaporated milk
1 egg, slightly beaten
1 cup soda cracker crumbs, crushed
2 T onion, diced
1 tsp. salt
1 tsp. dry ground mustard
1 T ketchup
6 to 8 American cheese slices

MAKES 6 SERVINGS

Blend all of the ingredients except the cheese. Line a loaf pan with wax paper. Put half of the cheese slices in bottom of pan. Cover with half of the meat mixture. Repeat layers.

Bake in 350° oven for 1 hour. Allow loaf to stand for 10 minutes before turning out onto a platter. Remove wax paper; slice for serving.

If in Doubt—Throw it Out!

What's the rule of thumb on leftovers? The general rule is to store for 3 days, throw it out on day 4. Here are a couple other words of advice:

• Store food in smaller portions in airtight containers and allow the steam to stop rising before chilling so you do not heat up the other food in the refrigerator.

• Get the food in the refrigerator within 2 hours after it's cooked or sooner if cooled.

Exceptions to the rule:
• Hard boiled eggs = keep 1 week
• Hard cheeses (cheddar, Swiss) = 3 to 4 weeks after opening
• Soft cheeses (brie, feta) = 1 week after opening
• Commercial mayonnaise = 2 months after opening

PREP TIME: COOK:
10 MINUTES   *10 MINUTES*

OVEN: *400°*   BAKE: *15 MINUTES*

¾ lb. lean ground beef

1 8 oz. pkg. mushrooms, sliced

½ medium red onion, cut into thin wedges

¼ tsp. kosher salt

¼ tsp. freshly ground black pepper

1 pkg. refrigerated pizza dough

3 oz. blue cheese, crumbled

fresh oregano to taste, chopped (optional)

BEEF MUSHROOM & ONION PIZZA

MAKES 4 SERVINGS

In a large skillet, cook beef, mushrooms, and onions over medium heat until beef is browned and onion is tender; drain off any fat; season with salt and pepper.

Line a large baking sheet with parchment paper. Unroll pizza dough on baking sheet and roll or pat down to about a 12" x 15" rectangle.

Top the dough with beef mixture keeping it 1 inch away from all edges. Bake pizza at 400° for 15 minutes or until crust is golden. Sprinkle pizza with blue cheese and oregano if desired.

TIP: *Substitute the blue cheese with gorgonzola cheese for a slightly milder taste.*

Sensational!

MOM'S LASAGNA

2 lbs. lean ground beef
¾ cup sweet onion, chopped
2 T olive oil
1 16 oz. can whole tomatoes, drained, broken-up
2 6 oz. cans tomato paste
2 cups water
¼ cup fresh parsley, chopped
2 tsp. kosher salt or to taste
1 tsp. sugar
1 tsp. garlic powder
½ tsp. black ground pepper
½ tsp. dried oregano
4 oz. lasagna noodles
1 15 oz. tub Italian ricotta cheese
2 cups mozzarella, shredded
1 cup parmesan cheese, grated

MAKES 8 SERVINGS

Lightly brown ground beef and onion in olive oil; chopping beef into small pieces. Add whole tomatoes, tomato paste, water, and all the seasonings to beef mixture.

Simmer uncovered, for about 30 minutes, stirring occasionally. Meanwhile, cook the lasagna noodles per package instructions. Rinse and leave in cold water. In a 9"x 13" baking dish, spread 1 cup of sauce, lift lasagna noodles from water, letting it drain, then layer on top of sauce (cut to fit pan if necessary). Add more sauce; top with cheeses. Continue to layer until there are 3 layers of each, ending with a layer of cheese.

Bake at 350° for 40 to 50 minutes or until lasagna top is browned. Let stand for 15 minutes before cutting into squares.

MMMMMMozzarella!

PREP TIME:  COOK: 20-
5 MINUTES   25 MINUTES

1 lb. lean ground beef
½ cup onion, diced
½ cup green pepper, diced
1 10¾ oz. can beef with
    barley condensed soup
¼ cup water
¼ cup ketchup
¼ tsp. dry ground mustard

SLOPPY JOES

MAKES 4 SERVINGS

In a medium skillet, cook beef, onion, and green pepper over medium-high heat until beef is browned and vegetables are soft. Add remaining ingredients; simmer for 15 minutes.

PREP TIME: COOK:
10 MINUTES   1 HOUR

2 slices bacon, cooked,
    diced
½ lb. ground beef
4 oz. medium egg noodles,
    cooked
1 green pepper, diced
1 onion, diced
1 28 oz. can whole
    tomatoes, broken-up
½ cup chili sauce
Kosher salt and black
    pepper to taste
dash of Tabasco hot pepper
    sauce, optional

SPANISH NOODLES

MAKES 6 SERVINGS

Brown beef in a large skillet until lightly browned. Add onion and green pepper and continue to cook until onion is softened, about 7 minutes. Add remaining ingredients, heat to a boil, cover, and reduce heat to low for 35 to 40 minutes.

CHAPTER NINE

HERE'S THE BEEF
FOR THE RED MEAT LOVER

PREP TIME: BAKE:
25 MINUTES *10 MINUTES*
OVEN: *425°* SET: *15 MINUTES*

1 8 to 12 oz. filet mignon
½ tsp. kosher salt
½ tsp. black pepper
½ tsp. dried oregano
1 T vegetable oil
1 large onion, thinly sliced
1 T balsamic vinegar
½ tsp. sugar (optional)
1 8 oz. pkg. refrigerated
   crescent rolls
2 oz. liver or truffle pate
1 egg white, beaten

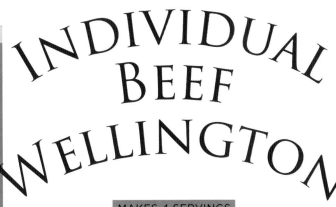

INDIVIDUAL BEEF WELLINGTON

MAKES 4 SERVINGS

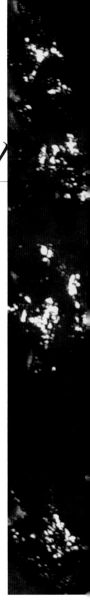

Cut filet into 4 equal pieces. Lightly season beef on all sides with salt, pepper, and oregano. In a large skillet, heat vegetable oil over medium-high heat. Sear beef on all sides. Transfer beef to a plate and let rest for 15 minutes.

Sauté sliced onions for 7 to 8 minutes or until soft. Add balsamic vinegar and sugar; continue to cook until onions are caramelized.

Unroll crescent rolls, do not divide into triangles; divide into 4 rectangles. Spread rectangles with pate. Place a filet in the center of each square and top with caramelized onions. Fold each corner up into center, layering like flower petals; pinch center to seal and cut vent slits for venting. Lightly brush top with egg white. Place pastries on a lightly greased rack that will fit into a shallow baking dish. Preheat oven to 425° and bake for 10 minutes or until crust is golden. Let rest 15 minutes.

BARBECUED BEEF

PREP TIME: 10 MINUTES   COOK: 15 MINUTES

OVEN: 350°   BAKE: 2 HOURS

3 to 4 lb. bottom or top round roast
½ tsp. ground black pepper
3 tsp. kosher salt, divided
¾ cup onion, chopped
2 T vegetable oil
1½ cup water
½ cup ketchup
1 14.5 oz. can tomato sauce
1 6 oz. can tomato paste
½ cup fresh lemon juice
3 T sugar
3 T Worcestershire sauce
3 T prepared mustard

MAKES 8 SERVINGS

Press pepper and 1 teaspoon of salt into the sides of roast. In a roasting pot or oven proof pan, brown the beef in oil; remove roast to plate and set aside. Add onion into the pot and cook until soft. Gradually add remaining ingredients; mixing until well blended. Place the roast back into pot, cover and place in 350° oven for 2 hours or until meat pulls apart with a fork.

Southern barbecue is the closest thing we have in the U.S. to Europe's wines and cheeses; drive a hundred miles and the barbecue changes. —Author, John Shelton Reed

VEAL SCALLOPINI

PREP TIME: 5 MINUTES   COOK: 4 MINUTES

OVEN: 325°   BAKE: 45 MINUTES

4 to 6 veal cutlets, thinly sliced
2 T flour
1 T vegetable oil
1 T butter
1 cup fresh mushrooms, sliced
1 tsp. fresh parsley, chopped
2 tsp. dried basil
1 14.5 oz. can whole tomatoes, drained, broken-up
⅛ tsp. garlic powder
2 T Parmesan cheese, grated

MAKES 4-6 SERVINGS

Lightly coat the cutlets with flour and brown in skillet with oil and butter. Place browned cutlets in a small greased casserole dish. Top cutlets with mushrooms, sprinkle with herbs, top with tomatoes, sprinkle with garlic powder, and top with cheese. Cover and bake at 325° for 45 minutes.

PREP TIME: *5 MINUTES*   COOK: *5-10 MINUTES*

OVEN: *325°*   BAKE: *3 HOURS*

3 lb. pot roast
kosher salt & black pepper
   to taste
1 T vegetable oil
1 10¾ oz. can French
   onion soup
¼ cup water
½ lb. potatoes, quartered
5 carrots, quartered
¼ cup flour
¼ cup water

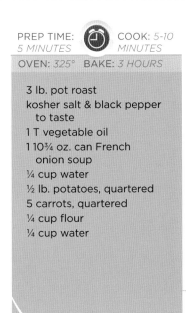

POT ROAST WITH ONION GRAVY

MAKES 6 SERVINGS

Press salt and pepper onto all sides of roast. In large roasting pot, brown pot roast in vegetable oil on all sides. Add onion soup and water; cover and bake at 325° for 2 hours. Add carrots, potatoes, and season with salt and pepper if needed. Cover and cook an additional 1 hour.

Remove meat and vegetables from pot. Mix flour and water to form a paste. Add paste to broth gradually, stirring constantly, over medium heat until it reaches a boil and thickens. Serve on the side.

SAFE COOKING TEMPERATURES

The United States Department of Agriculture updated its recommendation on May 24, 2011 for a safe cooking or doneness temperature for all meats, including pork, roasts and chops from 165° to 145° and allowing the meat to "rest" for at least 3 minutes. The change does not apply to ground meats or for chicken which remain at 165°. —foodsafety.gov

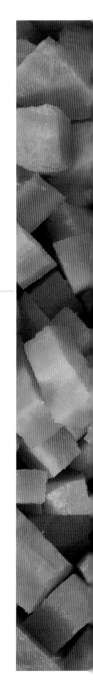

CARBONADE DE BEEF

PREP TIME: *10 MINUTES*   COOK: *15 MINUTES*

OVEN: *350°* BAKE: *2 HOURS*

2 to 2½ lb. beef rump roast
¼ cup flour
4 T butter, melted
1 cup beer
2 T white wine vinegar
2 10¾ oz. cans French onion soup
2 carrots, thinly sliced coins
1 tsp. sugar
¼ cup tomato sauce
1 tsp. dried celery flakes
1 tsp. dried parsley
1 bay leaf
¼ tsp. dried thyme

MAKES 8 SERVINGS

Cut beef into ½ inch thick serving size pieces and pound thin. Shake beef in flour. Melt butter over medium heat; lightly brown beef. Take meat out of pan and set aside. Drain off excess grease, if any. Deglaze pan with beer and add in vinegar, onion soup, carrots, sugar, tomato sauce, celery flakes, parsley, bay leaf, and thyme. Bring to boil and simmer 2 minutes. Place a layer of meat in a large casserole dish. Top with sauce then layer meat and sauce until dish is full. Cover tightly and bake at 350° for about 2 hours or meat is very tender.

TIP: *To save time, have your butcher cut the roast into ½ inch slices and run through a tenderizer.*

Tender!

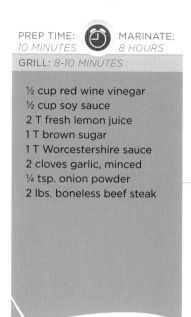

PREP TIME: *10 MINUTES*   MARINATE: *8 HOURS*

GRILL: *8-10 MINUTES*

½ cup red wine vinegar
½ cup soy sauce
2 T fresh lemon juice
1 T brown sugar
1 T Worcestershire sauce
2 cloves garlic, minced
¼ tsp. onion powder
2 lbs. boneless beef steak

BEEF MARINADE

MAKES 4 SERVINGS

Combine the first 7 ingredients in a large sealable plastic bag or airtight container. Add beef; seal bag and turn to coat. Refrigerate for 8 hours or overnight. Drain and discard marinade. Grill steak, covered over medium heat for 8 to 10 minutes or until desired doneness. Let stand 10 minutes before slicing.

GIVE IT A REST

Why wait for the meat to rest? During the "rest time" the temperature increases destroying pathogens. The juices also go back into the meat, leaving moist and favorable meat to enjoy. A few cuts of meat like fish, ribs, and chicken parts do not have enough meat mass to hold any residual heat so there is very little carry-over cooking. These meats do not need to rest and are best if eaten immediately. Here's a general rule of thumb for safe resting periods:

Steaks, thin chops, and whole chickens = 5 minutes
Thick chops, small roasts, rib roast, prime rib = 15 minutes
Whole turkey = 20 minutes
Pork butt and brisket = 30 minutes

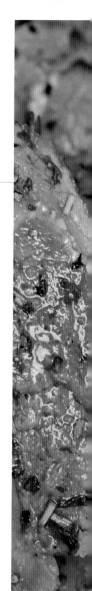

STEAK WITH MUSHROOMS

MAKES 4-6 SERVINGS

PREP TIME: *10 MINUTES*   COOK: *5 MINUTES*

OVEN: *350°* BAKE: *45 MINUTES*

¼ cup flour
½ tsp. kosher salt
¼ tsp. freshly ground black pepper
1½ lb. round steak
2 T vegetable oil
1 10¾ oz. can cream of mushroom soup
¼ cup milk or water
½ tsp. Worcestershire sauce
1 4 oz. can mushrooms, stems & pieces, drained

Cut steak into serving size pieces. Combine flour, salt, and pepper and pound flour mixture into meat. Brown the steak in oil and transfer to a 2 quart baking dish; set aside.

In a small bowl, combine mushroom soup, water, Worcestershire sauce, and mushrooms; mix well. Pour soup mixture over steak, cover and bake at 350° for 45 minutes.

THE BIG THAW

Have you ever pulled something out of the freezer and decided to defrost it fast in hot water or left food out on the counter to thaw? Neither method is considered a safe way to defrost meat. Bacteria begin to multiply when meat reaches 40°. Here are 4 safe ways to defrost meat:

• Refrigerator—It's best to plan ahead and thaw meat in the fridge. Thawed meats stay good for at least 3 days after thawing.

• Cold Water—Submerge meat in an airtight bag into cold water and change the water every 30 minutes. It should take about 1 hour per pound of meat.

• Microwave—Safe but plan to cook the food immediately after thawing.

• Cooking Frozen—Safe but the cooking time takes about 50% longer.

PREP TIME: *15 MINUTES*   COOK: *15 MINUTES*

OVEN: *350°*   BAKE: *2 HOURS*

3 T flour, divided
⅛ tsp. ground black pepper
1½ tsp. kosher salt, divided
1½ lb. round steak, 1" thick
¼ cup onion, diced
4 T butter, divided
½ cup tomato juice
2¼ cup wild rice, cooked
¼ cup fresh parsley, chopped
½ cup water

STEAK WITH WILD RICE

MAKES 4-6 SERVINGS

Combine 2 tablespoons of flour with pepper and 1 teaspoon of salt. Cut steak into serving size pieces. Pound the flour mixture into the meat on both sides; set aside.

Sauté onion in 2 tablespoons of butter until onion is almost transparent, about 7 to 8 minutes. Stir in the remaining flour and salt. Add tomato juice then cook over low heat stirring constantly for 7 to 8 minutes or until thickened.

Blend in rice and parsley; spread mixture on steak. Roll and fasten with skewers or kitchen twine. Brown meat in remaining butter using an oven proof pan; add water. Cover and bake at 350° for about 2 hours or until meat is tender.

Pound and sauté!

STEAK & PEPPER TACOS

MAKES 4 SERVINGS

PREP TIME: 15 MINUTES   MARINATE: 30 MINUTES

COOK: 16 MINUTES
REST: 10 MINUTES

- 1 lb. flank or hanger steak
- juice of 1 lime + wedges for serving
- 1 tsp. kosher salt
- 2 cloves garlic, crushed
- ½ tsp. mild chili powder
- 3 T vegetable oil, divided
- ½ red onion, thinly sliced
- 3 bell peppers, 1 of each color
- ½ cup fresh or frozen corn kernels
- 8 small corn tortillas, warmed
- ½ avocado, sliced
- ¼ cup Monterey Jack cheese, shredded
- ¼ cup salsa Verde or 2 T fresh cilantro
- 2 T sliced pickled jalapeños
- sour cream (optional)

Marinate steak in lime juice, salt, garlic, and chili powder in a sealable plastic bag for 30 minutes. Meanwhile, heat 1 tablespoon of oil in a large skillet. Cook red onion and peppers, tossing frequently for 5 minutes. Add the corn and continue to cook until the peppers are charred and soft, about 3 minutes. Transfer vegetables to a bowl and keep warm.

Add remaining oil to skillet. Remove steak from marinade and pat dry. Lay the steak in pan and cook over medium-high heat, turning once, for 8 minutes (for medium-rare). Transfer to cutting board; let rest for 10 minutes. Slice steak across the grain and arrange on a platter with the peppers and lime wedges. Make the tacos with meat, peppers, warm tortillas, avocado, cheese, salsa, jalapeños, and sour cream.

PREP TIME:
15 MINUTES

BAKE:
15 MINUTES

2 T olive oil, divided
2 12 oz. boneless strip
  steaks
¼ tsp. kosher salt
⅛ tsp. black pepper
2 cups mushrooms, sliced
1 large shallot, chopped
2 cloves garlic, minced
2 oz. brandy
1 cup beef broth
1 T cornstarch
2 T fresh parsley, chopped

STRIP STEAK DIANE

MAKES 4 SERVINGS

Heat 1 tablespoon of oil in a large skillet (not non-stick) over medium-high heat. Season the steaks with salt and pepper. Add to skillet and sauté for 4 minutes per side; remove steaks to a plate, loosely cover and let rest.

Add remaining oil to skillet. Stir in mushrooms, shallots, and garlic; cook 3 minutes, stirring occasionally. Remove from heat; add brandy. Return to heat and scrape browned bits from bottom; cook 1 minute.

Combine broth and cornstarch; add to mushroom mixture and cook 1 to 2 minutes, until thickened. Stir in parsley. Thinly slice the steak and serve with mushroom sauce.

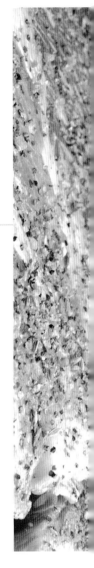

RICE STUFFED FRANKFURTERS

PREP TIME: 5 MINUTES
BAKE: 20 MINUTES
OVEN: 350°

1½ lbs. beef frankfurters
¼ cup Dijon mustard
1 pkg. Spanish rice mix, prepared
½ cup cheddar cheese

MAKES 6 SERVINGS

Split frankfurters lengthwise without cutting all the way through. Spread mustard on inside surfaces of frankfurters. Place in a large, lightly greased, shallow baking dish.

Fill each frankfurter with about ⅓ cup of the prepared Spanish rice; sprinkle with cheese. Bake uncovered, in oven at 350° for 20 minutes.

CORN BEEF CASSEROLE

PREP TIME: 10 MINUTES
BAKE: 30 MINUTES
OVEN: 350°

½ lb. corn beef, deli sliced
1 16 oz. pkg. frozen mixed vegetables, cooked
1 10¾ oz. can cream of mushroom soup
2 T water
½ cup Velveeta pasteurized processed cheese, cubed
½ cup potato chips, crumbled

MAKES 4 SERVINGS

Press corn beef against sides and bottom of a lightly greased 1 quart casserole dish forming a lining. Place vegetables in center. Mix mushroom soup with water and pour over top. Scatter top with cheese and top with potato chips.

Bake casserole in oven at 350° for 30 minutes or until cheese is melted and bubbling.

CHAPTER TEN

SOMETHING TO CROW ABOUT
CHICKEN, TURKEY, & OTHER FOWL

BASIL GRILLED CHICKEN

MAKES 4 SERVINGS

GRILL: *MEDIUM*

- ¾ tsp. freshly black pepper, ground, divided
- 4 skinless chicken breast halves
- ⅓ cup butter, melted
- ¼ cup + 2 T fresh basil, minced, divided
- ½ cup butter, softened
- 1 T Parmesan cheese, grated
- ¼ tsp. garlic powder
- ⅛ tsp. kosher salt
- ⅛ tsp. freshly ground black pepper

Press ½ teaspoon pepper into chicken breasts. Combine melted butter and ¼ cup basil; stir well and brush lightly over chicken. Grill chicken over medium heat, 8 to 10 minutes on each side, basting frequently with remaining melted butter mixture.

Combine softened butter, remaining basil, cheese, garlic powder, salt, and remaining pepper in a small bowl. Beat with mixer at low speed until mixture is smooth. Serve chicken with a small dollop of softened butter mixture on each breast.

PUT A LID ON IT!

One of the most important grilling rules is to keep the lid down. Lifting the lid allows the heat and moisture to escape and increases the grilling time. Open the lid only to flip the food. Also, do not pierce the meat or flip it repeatedly. It will not improve the taste.

Pass the pepper!

GINGER-ORANGE DUCK BREAST

PREP TIME: 10 MINUTES   COOK: 25-30 MINUTES

1 T olive oil
kosher salt & black pepper to taste
1 lb. boneless, skinless, duck breasts
½ cup onion, minced
1 T fresh ginger, minced
1 cup low sodium chicken broth
¼ cup orange marmalade
1 T grated orange peel
2 tsp. fresh parsley, finely chopped
white or brown rice, cooked

MAKES 4 SERVINGS

In a medium skillet, heat up olive oil. Lightly salt and pepper duck breast and brown for 7 minutes on each side or until internal temperature reaches 165°. Remove breasts from pan, thinly slice, and keep warm. In the same skillet, sauté onion and ginger for 1 minute. Add chicken broth and marmalade. Bring to a boil, then simmer for 10 minutes or until sauce has reduced to 1 cup. Stir in orange peel and parsley; cook 1 minute. Serve sauce with warm duck over rice.

BAKED CHICKEN

PREP TIME: 10 MINUTES   BAKE: 50-55 MINUTES
OVEN: 350°

5 T butter, melted, divided (½ stick)
4 boneless, skinless chicken breast halves
1 8 oz. pkg. slices Swiss cheese
1 10 ¾ oz. can cream of chicken soup
¼ cup milk
1 cup stuffing mix

MAKES 4 SERVINGS

Coat the bottom of a 9" x 13" casserole dish with 2 tablespoons of butter. Cut chicken into serving size pieces and place in dish; top with cheese slices. Mix soup with milk; spread evenly over top of cheese. Sprinkle in stuffing mix and bake uncovered at 350° for 55 minutes.

TIP: *This recipe has been a family favorite. Jazz it up a little with jalapeño peppers or green chilies. Also try adding 2 tablespoons of chopped almonds to the stuffing mix.*

TERIYAKI GRILLED CHICKEN

PREP TIME: *10 MINUTES*   MARINATE: *5 HOURS*

GRILL: *MEDIUM*
COOK: *20 MINUTES*

⅓ cup soy sauce
¼ cup canola oil
2 green onions, thinly sliced
2 T honey
2 T sherry or chicken broth
2 cloves garlic, minced
1 tsp. fresh ginger root, minced
6 bone-in chicken breast halves

MAKES 6 SERVINGS

Combine the first 7 ingredients in a large sealable plastic bag or airtight container. Add the chicken, turn to coat and refrigerate for at least 5 hours. Drain and discard marinade.

Prepare grill for indirect heat, using a drip pan. Grill covered, over indirect medium heat for about 20 minutes turning after 10 minutes or until a meat thermometer reads 165°.

GRILLING TIPS

• *Take the meat out of the fridge at least 45 minutes before cooking. Cold meat reduces the grill temperature, makes the meat stick and prevents the juices from getting seared into the meat.*

• *Use tongs instead of a fork. Piercing with a fork allows the juices to flow out leaving a dried and tough piece of meat.*

• *If basting with sauce, separate the basting sauce before marinating and from the serving sauce. Do not baste until the last few minutes of grilling. Most sauces contain sugar which will cause burning.*

PREP TIME: BAKE:
10 MINUTES 15 MINUTES
OVEN: 350°

½ cup cream cheese
1 13 oz. can chicken breast, drained
1 T onion, diced
1 T sesame seeds, toasted
½ tsp. dried parsley
kosher salt & black pepper to taste
1 8 oz. pkg. refrigerated crescent rolls

CHICKEN POPOVERS

MAKES 4 SERVINGS

Combine cream cheese, chicken breast, sesame seeds, parsley, and onion; mix well. Unroll crescent rolls, do not divide into triangles, divide into 4 rectangles. Place rectangles onto a lightly greased baking sheet. Press flat and pinch the perforated diagonal seam together to close. Place about ¼ cup of chicken mixture in center of each rectangle. Fold each corner up into center, layering like flower petals; pinch center to seal. Bake in 350° oven for 15 minutes or until golden brown.

TIP: *This recipe is a tad messy to eat but it is delicious and is a great choice for a healthy lunch.*

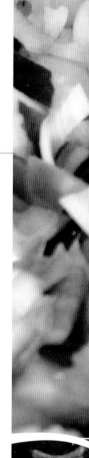

PREP TIME: MARINATE:
10 MINUTES 1-2 HOURS
GRILL: MEDIUM
COOK: 10 MINUTES

1 tsp. lime peel, grated
½ cup fresh lime juice
1 T ground allspice
1 T light brown sugar
1 to 2 T jalapeño pepper, chopped
2 T olive oil
1 tsp. kosher salt
1 tsp. freshly ground black pepper
1 tsp. dried thyme
1 tsp. ground cinnamon
½ tsp. ground nutmeg
½ cup onion, chopped
1 lb. skinless, boneless chicken thighs
½ lb. skinless, boneless chicken breasts

JERK-STYLE CHICKEN

MAKES 6 SERVINGS

Combine the first 11 ingredients in a blender; process until well blended. Pour into an air tight container or sealable plastic bag; add the onion and chicken. Marinate for 1 to 2 hours, turning occasionally. Remove chicken from bag or container, discarding the marinade. Grill chicken over medium heat covered for 5 minutes on each side or until done.

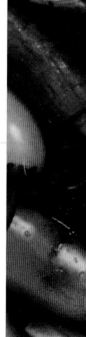

CHICKEN IN LETTUCE CUPS

PREP TIME: 15 MINUTES   COOK: 10 MINUTES

- 3 T reduced-sodium soy sauce
- 2 tsp. fresh ginger, peeled, grated
- 1 tsp. honey
- 2 tsp. Asian sesame oil
- 1¼ lbs. chicken tenders, cut into ¼" pieces
- 1 cup frozen shelled edamame (soy beans)
- 2 medium stalks celery, chopped
- 12 large Boston lettuce leaves

MAKES 4 SERVINGS

Combine soy sauce, ginger, and honey; set aside. In a 12 inch non-stick skillet, heat sesame oil on medium heat. Add chicken; cook 3 minutes, stirring occasionally. Add edamame and celery to chicken; continue to cook for 2 minutes. Add in soy sauce mixture; cook for 2 minutes or until chicken is cooked through, stirring occasionally to coat chicken with sauce. Arrange lettuce leaves on 4 plates. Divide about ¼ cup of chicken mixture among each lettuce leaf. Wrap leaves over chicken and eat out of hand.

TIP: *Jazz this recipe up with your favorite seasonings or add a few chopped jalapeño peppers for a little extra heat.*

PREP TIME: COOK:
5 MINUTES   14 MINUTES

MARINATE: *1-4 HOURS*

⅔ cup soy sauce
¼ cup orange juice
2 T fresh lime juice
2 large garlic cloves, pressed
4 boneless chicken breast halves

GOLDEN CITRUS BROILED CHICKEN

MAKES 4 SERVINGS

In a large food storage bag, combine soy sauce, orange juice, lime juice, and garlic. Add chicken, press air out of the bag and secure top. Turn bag over several times to coat chicken. Marinate for 1 to 4 hours in refrigerator. Remove chicken from bag and discard marinade. Broil chicken 5 inches from broiler for 8 minutes. Turn breasts over and cook 6 minutes longer or until chicken is no longer pink in the middle.

TIP: *This is a fast and easy recipe to prepare. A great tasting recipe served for lunch over salad greens.*

Fresh and tasty!

OVEN ROASTED CHICKEN & POTATOES

PREP TIME: 15 MINUTES
COOK: 90 MINUTES

OVEN: 375°

- 1 to 3½ lb. chicken, cut-up
- 6 potatoes, peeled, cut into quarters
- 1 head garlic, cloves peeled, halved
- 1 cup low-salt chicken broth
- kosher salt and black pepper to taste
- ¾ cup extra virgin olive oil
- 1 cup fresh lemon juice (about 3 to 4 lemons)
- 3 tsp. dried oregano, crumbled

MAKES 4-6 SERVINGS

Arrange chicken, potatoes, and garlic in a large roasting pan. Pour broth over top and season with salt and pepper. Whisk together oil, lemon juice, and oregano and pour evenly over chicken and potatoes. Bake chicken in 375° oven for 90 minutes or until chicken is cooked through and golden brown.

TIP: *I like to mix up the potatoes with a combination of Yukon golds, reds, and fingerlings. Cut into evenly sized chunks to assure even cooking.*

PREP TIME: 5 MINUTES   COOK: 15 MINUTES

OVEN: 450°
BAKE: 1 HOUR, 20 MINUTES

¼ cup onion, chopped
½ cup celery, chopped
¼ cup butter, melted
¼ tsp. kosher salt
½ tsp. poultry seasoning
½ cup chicken stock
1¼ cups corn flake crumbs
   (5 cups flakes)
1 2½ to 3 lb. whole chicken
1 15 oz. can peach halves,
   syrup reserved

PEACH ROASTED CHICKEN

MAKES 4 SERVINGS

Melt butter in a large skillet. Add onion and celery and cook until almost tender. Add seasonings and stock. Remove from heat and lightly toss in the corn flake crumbs. Stuff mixture into chicken cavity and truss closed.

Place chicken on a 24 inch long piece of aluminum foil. Brush with reserved peach syrup. Double fold ends and sides of foil. Place in a roasting pan and roast in oven at 450° for 1 hour.

Open foil and flatten in pan. Place peach halves on foil around the chicken and baste with drippings. Return to oven and roast for an additional 20 minutes.

LEMON & HERB ROASTED CHICKEN

PREP TIME: 15 MINUTES

BAKE: 55-60 MINUTES

OVEN: 450°, 375°

- ½ cup (1 stick) butter, softened
- 2 T fresh rosemary, chopped or 2 tsp. dried
- 2 T fresh thyme, chopped or 2 tsp. dried
- 3 garlic cloves, minced
- 1½ tsp. lemon peel, grated
- kosher salt & black pepper to taste
- 1 3 to 4 lb. whole chicken
- ¼ cup dry white wine
- 1 cup low-salt chicken broth
- 2 T all-purpose flour
- lemon wedges (optional)
- rosemary sprigs (optional)

MAKES 6-8 SERVINGS

Combine butter, rosemary, thyme, garlic, and lemon peel. Season mixture with salt and pepper to taste. Slide hand under skin to loosen. Spread butter mixture under and over skin reserving 2 tablespoons for gravy. Preheat oven to 450°. Roast chicken on a rack in a roasting pan for 20 minutes. Reduce temperature to 375° and continue to roast until meat reaches 165° internal temperature, about 35 to 40 minutes. Let rest at least 5 minutes.

TURKEY PLEASURE

PREP TIME: 15 MINUTES

BAKE: 55 MINUTES

OVEN: 350°

- 4 whole potatoes, cooked, sliced thin
- 2 cups turkey breast, cooked, diced
- ¼ cup butter, melted
- 2 tsp. paprika
- ½ tsp. kosher salt
- ⅛ tsp. black pepper
- ¼ tsp. thyme
- 1 cup turkey or chicken broth
- 1 cup cheddar cheese, shredded

MAKES 4 SERVINGS

Place half of the potatoes in a greased 2 quart casserole dish. Cover with half of the diced turkey then add remaining potatoes. Top with remaining turkey. Combine butter, paprika, salt, pepper, and thyme. Mix into broth. Pour over turkey and potatoes, cover and bake at 350° for 40 minutes. Uncover, sprinkle cheese on top and bake for another 15 minutes.

PREP TIME: BAKE:
5 MINUTES 50 MINUTES
OVEN: 375°

1 10¾ oz. can cream of
  chicken soup
1⅓ cups water
¾ cup long-grain white rice,
  uncooked
½ tsp. onion powder
½ tsp. kosher salt
¼ tsp. black pepper
2 cups frozen mixed
  vegetables
4 skinless chicken breast
  halves
½ cup cheddar cheese,
  finely shredded

CHEESY CHICKEN & RICE CASSEROLE

MAKES 4 SERVINGS

Mix together soup, water, rice, onion powder, salt, pepper, and vegetables in a 2 quart baking dish. Top with chicken. Cover and bake at 375° for 50 minutes or until chicken and rice are done. Top with cheese and let stand a few minutes before serving.

PREP TIME:  COOK:
15 MINUTES 10 MINUTES
OVEN: 400° BAKE: 40 MINUTES

1 T butter
2 T flour
1 cup chicken broth
1 cup milk
1½ tsp. celery salt
freshly ground black
  pepper to taste
½ lb. wide noodles, cooked,
  drained
2 chicken breasts, cooked
1 4 oz. can mushrooms,
  drained
1 8 oz. can tomato sauce
6 T tomato paste (½ 6 oz.
  can)
½ cup Romano cheese,
  grated

CHICKEN TETRAZZINI

MAKES 4 SERVINGS

Melt butter in large skillet on medium heat. Add in flour stirring constantly until combined. Mix together chicken broth, milk, celery salt, and pepper. Gradually add mixture into butter and flour stirring constantly to make a cream sauce. Add noodles, chicken breasts, and mushrooms.

Pour into a greased 2 quart casserole. Mix tomatoes with the tomato paste and spread on top of casserole. Top with cheese. Bake at 400° for 40 minutes.

CHICKEN ENCHILADA PIZZA

OVEN: *425°*

- 1 13.8 oz. pkg. refrigerated pizza dough
- ½ cup enchilada sauce (½ can)
- 1 cup cheddar-jack cheese, shredded
- 1 15.5 oz. can mild chili beans, drained
- ¾ lb. chicken breast, cooked
- ½ cup pickled jalapeno slices

MAKES 4 SERVINGS

Roll pizza dough onto a lightly greased cookie sheet and pre-bake in 425° oven for 8 minutes. Spread enchilada sauce over crust to within 1 inch from the edges. Evenly scatter the chicken, beans, and peppers over sauce and top with cheese. Bake pizza at 425° for 16 to 17 minutes or until crust is golden brown.

TIP: *You can substitute the cooked chicken breast with one 13 oz. can chicken breast. Spice it up by substituting medium or hot chili beans. Top with fresh tomatoes, sour cream, and olive slices.*

PREP TIME: *5 MINUTES*   BAKE: *1½ HOURS*

OVEN: *300°*

3 T lemon pepper seasoning
3 T garlic salt
1 T onion powder
1 T dried whole thyme
1 4 to 6 lb. turkey breast
large paper bag

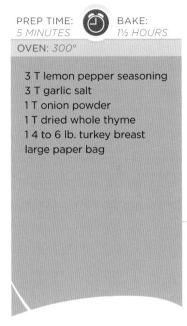

SEASONED TURKEY BREAST

MAKES 4-6 SERVINGS

Combine first 4 ingredients in a small bowl; set aside. Remove the skin from turkey breast and pat dry with a paper towel. Coat the turkey liberally with cooking spray. Sprinkle seasoning mixture over turkey, coating thoroughly; Set aside.

Coat the inside of paper bag with non-stick cooking spray and place turkey inside. Fold ends of bag under and place in a broiler pan coated with cooking spray. Bake at 300° for 1 hour and 30 minutes or about 22 minutes per pound.

MYTH BUSTER

Myth—The pilgrims ate turkey and pumpkin pie to celebrate their arrival to the New World and we've been celebrating it ever since.

Truth—Abraham Lincoln declared Thanksgiving a national holiday in 1863. The pilgrims did not eat turkey or pumpkin pie.

MOIST TURKEY BURGERS

⅓ cup onion, diced
2 tsp. canola oil, divided
½ cup soft bread crumbs
½ tsp. lite soy sauce
½ tsp. Worcestershire sauce
¼ tsp. garlic powder
¼ tsp. poultry seasoning
⅛ tsp. ground mustard
⅛ tsp. black pepper
dash of kosher salt
½ lb. lean ground turkey
2 hamburger buns (optional)
2 lettuce leaves (optional)
2 tomato slices (optional)

MAKES 2 SERVINGS

Place onion and ½ teaspoon oil in a small skillet; cover and cook for 3 to 4 minutes or until soft. Remove from heat; cool.

In a large bowl, combine bread crumbs, soy sauce, Worcestershire sauce, garlic powder, poultry seasoning, mustard, pepper, and salt. Crumble turkey over mixture and mix just until combined. Shape into 2 patties. Wrap in plastic and refrigerate for 20 minutes.

Heat remaining oil in a non-stick skillet; cook patties over medium heat for 4 to 5 minutes on each side or until meat thermometer reads 165°. Serve on buns with lettuce and tomato if desired.

Nutritious!

PREP TIME: *15 MINUTES*   COOK: *10 MINUTES*

OVEN: *450°*   BAKE: *5 MINUTES*

1 T vegetable oil

1 lb. turkey breast, cubed small

1 16 oz. pkg. frozen peppers & onion stir-fry vegetables

1 10 oz. can enchilada sauce

½ cup canned whole cranberry sauce

kosher salt to taste

black pepper to taste

9 6-inch corn tortillas, halved

1 8 oz. pkg. Mexican blend shredded cheese

Lime wedges (optional)

CRAN-TURKEY ENCHILADAS

MAKES 4 SERVINGS

Heat oil in a large skillet over medium heat; cook turkey for about 4 minutes or until no longer pink, stirring occasionally. Add stir-fry vegetables, enchilada sauce, and cranberry sauce; bring to boil. Remove skillet from heat and season with salt and pepper to taste.

In a 2 quart baking dish layer ⅓ of tortillas, then top with ⅓ of cheese. Using a slotted spoon, add layer with ½ of turkey mixture. Add another layer of ⅓ of tortillas, ⅓ of cheese and remaining turkey mixture (using slotted spoon). Add remaining tortillas, pour sauce from skillet over tortillas and top with remaining cheese.

Bake uncovered in 450° oven for 5 minutes or until heated through and cheese melts. Cut into 4 squares. Serve with lime wedge if desired.

HONEY-GLAZED CORNISH HENS

2 1½ lb. Cornish game hens
1 tsp. fresh orange peel, grated
¼ cup orange juice concentrate, thawed, undiluted
3 T fresh lemon juice
2 T soy sauce
2 cloves garlic, crushed, minced
1 T honey
½ tsp. onion powder
¼ tsp. dried thyme
½ cup chopped onion
fresh orange wedges (optional)
1 tsp. cornstarch
1 tsp. cold water

MAKES 2 SERVINGS

Place game hens breast side down on a cutting board and cut in half along backbone. Remove skin and trim excess fat. In small micro-safe dish, combine orange peel, lemon juice, orange juice concentrate, soy sauce, honey, garlic, onion powder, and thyme. Bring to a boil in microwave; set aside.

Lightly grease a large baking dish. Divide onions into 4 portions in baking dish; place hens bone side down on onions. Pour orange juice mixture over hens.

Bake hens in 350° oven for 45 minutes, basting every 10 to 15 minutes with cooking juices. If they brown too quickly, cover loosely with foil. Remove hens and onions to serving plates.

Skim fat off remaining juices in baking dish. Pour juices into sauce pan. Combine cornstarch and water. Add to juices over medium heat, stirring constantly, until thickened. Serve sauce on the side.

CHAPTER ELEVEN

The Other White Meat
PORK CHOPS, TENDERLOIN, RIBS, HAM, BACON, & SAUSAGE

MUSTARD GLAZED PORK CHOPS
PORK CHOPS & RICE
RED BEANS & RICE
PORK CHOPS AGRO DOLCE
PORK SALTIMBOCCA
PORK TENDERLOIN WITH PRUNES
SPECIAL BARBECUED RIBS
SWEET JALAPEÑO RIBS
STICKY SWEET RIBS
HAM & SWEET POTATO CASSEROLE
SAUSAGE STUFFED SHELLS
RICE-FILLED HAM POCKETS
BACON & BLUE CHEESE TARTS

MUSTARD GLAZED PORK CHOPS

PREP TIME: 5 MINUTES COOK: *16-20 MINUTES*

4 bone-in pork chops, ½" thick
2 tsp. olive oil
1 large onion, cut in thin wedges
½ cup apricot preserves
1 T Dijon or spicy mustard
¼ cup water
1 tsp. paprika
½ tsp. ground nutmeg

MAKES 4 SERVINGS

Season chops with salt and pepper. In a large skillet, heat olive oil over medium-high heat. Add pork and onions and cook 3 to 4 minutes. Turn chops and onions and cook an additional 3 to 4 minutes.

Meanwhile, combine the preserves, mustard, water, paprika, and nutmeg in a micro-safe bowl. Heat mixture in the microwave for 1 to 2 minutes or until melted. Pour mixture over pork and onions, reduce heat to medium, cover and cook 10 minutes.

LIVING HIGH ON THE HOG

The insinuation of the familiar phrase "high on the hog" is derived from the thought that the tastiest parts of the hog are its upper parts. So if you are living high on the hog, you've got the best life has to offer.

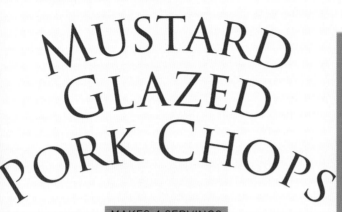

High on the hog!

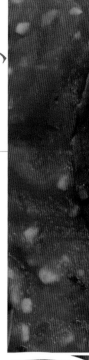

PREP TIME: 15 MINUTES COOK: 8 MINUTES
OVEN: 350° BAKE: 75 MINUTES

1 T olive oil
6 pork chops, 1" thick
kosher salt & black pepper to taste
1 cup long grain rice
2 T shortening
1 T onion, minced
⅛ tsp. garlic powder
1 8 oz. can tomato sauce
1½ cups water
½ cup cheddar cheese, shredded
½ tsp. kosher salt
dash of black pepper

PORK CHOPS & RICE

MAKES 6 SERVINGS

Heat olive oil in a large skillet over medium-high heat. Salt and pepper pork chops and brown for 3 to 4 minutes on each side. Remove from heat; set aside. In a medium bowl, mix together rice, shortening, onion, garlic powder, tomato sauce, water, cheese, salt, and pepper. Pour into a greased 2 quart baking dish. Arrange pork chops on top, cover and bake at 350° for 1 hour and 15 minutes or until chops are fork tender.

PREP TIME: 15 MINUTES  BAKE: 70 MINUTES

¾ lb. pork shoulder, cut into ½" cubes
1 cup onion, chopped
¾ cup green pepper, chopped
1 clove garlic, minced
1½ cups water
3 16 oz. cans red beans, drained
1 14.5 oz. can stewed tomatoes, chopped
1 6 oz. can tomato paste
¼ tsp. dried oregano
¼ tsp. dried thyme
¼ tsp. Tabasco hot pepper sauce
1 bay leaf
4 cups long-grain or Spanish rice, cooked
pickled jalapeño pepper slices (optional)

RED BEANS & RICE

MAKES 8 SERVINGS

Heat a lightly oiled Dutch oven over medium-high heat until hot. Add pork, onions, peppers, and garlic; sauté for 10 minutes or until vegetables are tender. Add water, scraping bottom and sides to clean pan. Add beans, tomatoes, water, tomato paste, oregano, thyme, hot sauce, and bay leaf.

Cover, reduce heat to simmer and cook for 1 hour, or until pork is tender, stirring occasionally. Remove and discard bay leaf. Serve over rice and top with jalapeño peppers if desired.

PORK CHOPS ARGO DOLCE

4 bone-in pork chops,
  1" thick
kosher salt & black pepper
  to taste
1 T olive oil
2 T honey
½ cup balsamic vinegar
1 tsp. fresh thyme
½ cup chicken broth
2 T butter

MAKES 4 SERVINGS

Season pork chops with salt and pepper. Warm the oil in a large skillet over medium-high heat. Add chops; cook, turning once, until golden brown, about 3 to 4 minutes per side. Transfer to plate, set aside.

Reduce heat to medium. Add honey, vinegar, and thyme to same skillet; cook until liquid is thickened and reduced by half, about 5 minutes. Stir in broth; bring to a simmer.

Return chops to pan; cover and cook 3 to 4 minutes. Uncover and cook, turning chops occasionally and basting with sauce for about 10 to 15 minutes. Transfer chops to plate, tent loosely with foil and let rest.

Increase heat to medium-high; simmer sauce until syrupy, about 3 minutes. Remove from heat, stir in butter until incorporated. Season sauce with salt and pepper to taste. Drizzle sauce over pork chops.

PREP TIME: 10 MINUTES COOK: 15 MINUTES

- 4 6 oz. boneless pork chops, ¾" thick
- kosher salt and black pepper to taste
- 8 fresh sage leaves
- 3 oz. Prosciutto, thinly sliced
- 2 T olive oil
- ½ cup beef broth
- 2 tsp. cornstarch
- ½ cup Marsala wine
- 1 cup Fontina cheese, shredded
- 1 prepared polenta roll, grilled (optional)

PORK SALTIMBOCCA

MAKES 6-8 SERVINGS

Season pork chops with salt and pepper. Place 2 sage leaves on each pork chop and top each with ¼ of prosciutto. With sharp side of chef's knife pointed up, gently pound pork so that prosciutto adheres to it. Heat oil in a large non-stick skillet over medium-high heat. Place pork, prosciutto side down, in skillet; cook for 3 to 4 minutes. Transfer chops to a plate.

Combine beef broth with cornstarch. In the skillet, combine broth mixture with Marsala wine, scraping up browned bits from the bottom. Add pork back into skillet, prosciutto side up and top each chop with ¼ of cheese. Cover and simmer for about 3 to 4 minutes or until the cheese melts and pork temperature reaches 155° if using thermometer. Top each chop with sauce and serve with grilled polenta if desired.

Cheese!

PORK TENDERLOIN WITH PRUNES

PREP TIME: BAKE:
20 MINUTES   40 MINUTES
OVEN: *400°*

1 to 1½ lbs. pork tenderloin
8 bay leaves
15 large prunes, pitted
kosher salt and black
　　pepper to taste

MAKES 6 SERVINGS

Place bay leaves and prunes in a bowl. Pour 1½ cups boiling water over the top and let sit for 15 minutes. Remove, pat dry; set aside.

Make a deep slit lengthwise on the tenderloin leaving about 1 inch un-cut on each end. Place prunes into the bottom of slit in tight row. Finely crumble 1 bay leaf and sprinkle over prunes. Roll meat and tie tightly with kitchen twine at 1 inch intervals. Sprinkle with salt and pepper. Place remaining leaves under the twine.

Place tenderloin on a lightly greased shallow baking pan. Bake for 30 to 35 minutes in 400° oven or until internal temperature reaches 150°. Place tenderloin on a platter, cover loosely with a foil tent, and let rest for 10 minutes before slicing.

PREP TIME: 5 MINUTES   COOK: 10 MINUTES
OVEN: 250°/400°
BAKE: 2½ HOURS

1 T celery seed
1 T chili powder
¼ cup brown sugar
1 T kosher salt
1 tsp. sweet paprika
2½ lbs. pork loin back ribs
1 8 oz. can tomato sauce
¼ cup vinegar

SPECIAL BARBECUED RIBS

MAKES 4 SERVINGS

Combine celery seed, chili powder, sugar, salt, and paprika. Rub ⅓ of mixture on ribs. Add tomato sauce and vinegar to the remaining mixture. Heat through and simmer on low for 10 minutes; set aside.

Place the meat into a 9"x 13" casserole dish. Add about 1 inch of water (or about halfway up each rib). Bake in 250° oven for 1 hour. Remove from oven, turn over meat and bake for 1 more hour.

Drain water, baste ribs with barbecue sauce; increase heat to 400°; bake for an additional 30 minutes.

RUB IT LIKE YOU LOVE IT

Here are a couple of tips to assure your ribs are tender and mouthwatering:

Remove the membrane off the back of the ribs. This is a bit of a hassle but worth the work. It will make the difference between a tough and tender meat.

When you add the seasonings to the meat, give it a good rub to get it into the meat and well dispersed. You won't be disappointed!

SWEET JALAPEÑO RIBS

MAKES 6 SERVINGS

PREP TIME: *10 MINUTES* COOK: *5 MINUTES*

OVEN: *375°/350°* BAKE: *2 HOURS*

3 lbs. country-style pork ribs, separated
1½ tsp. seasoning salt (see recipe below)
1 medium onion, thinly sliced
1 10 oz. jar mild or sweet jalapeño jelly
1 10 oz. bottle Heinz 57 sauce
1-2 jalapeño peppers, seeded, minced (optional)
Seasoning salt:
3 T kosher salt
1 T onion powder
2 T garlic powder
2 T paprika
1 T black pepper dash (or 2) cayenne pepper

Arrange ribs fat side down in a single layer on a greased shallow baking pan. Sprinkle with seasoned salt. Arrange sliced onions over ribs. Cover with foil and bake at 375° for 30 minutes. Reduce temperature to 350°, remove foil and bake 30 minutes longer. Drain and discard onion.

Meanwhile, heat jelly, Heinz 57 sauce, and jalapeño peppers in a small sauce pan, stirring constantly until well combined and jelly melts. Pour sauce over ribs, reserving some sauce to serve with ribs, and continue to bake an additional 50 to 60 minutes.

Seasoning salt: Combine all ingredients in an airtight container. Shake or stir until there is a uniform color.

TIP: *This sauce promises a sweet taste up front, finishing with a zesty bite of heat. Omit the jalapeño pepper for a milder sauce.*

PREP TIME: BAKE:
10 MINUTES   *2 HOURS*

OVEN: *350°*

- 3 lbs. pork loin back ribs
- 1 cup maple syrup
- 3 T frozen orange juice concentrate
- 3 T ketchup
- 2 T soy sauce
- 1 T Dijon mustard
- 1 T Worcestershire sauce
- 1 tsp. curry
- 1 clove garlic, minced
- 3 green onions, minced
- 1 T sesame seeds

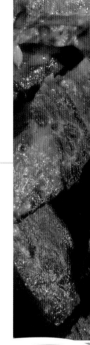

STICKY SWEET RIBS

MAKES 6 SERVINGS

Place ribs fat side down into a large baking pan. Cover and bake in oven 350° for 1 hour and 15 minutes. Meanwhile, combine remaining ingredients in a sauce pan. Heat sauce to a boil then simmer for 15 minutes. Remove ribs from oven, drain off any fat, and pour sauce over ribs, reserving some sauce for basting or serving. Bake uncovered, another 30 minutes.

PREP TIME:  COOK:
20 MINUTES   *10 MINUTES*

OVEN: *375°*   BAKE: *30 MINUTES*

- 1 ham slice (1 lb.), ¾" thick, cooked
- 2 small sweet potatoes
- 4 pineapple slices (½ can)
- 2 T milk
- ¼ tsp. cinnamon
- ¼ tsp. kosher salt
- ⅛ tsp. black pepper
- ½ cup cornflakes, crushed

HAM & SWEET POTATO CASSEROLE

MAKES 6 SERVINGS

Cut ham into 4 pieces and place in greased 1 quart casserole. Peel, quarter, and cook the sweet potatoes in boiling water for 10 minutes or until soft to the fork. Whip sweet potatoes with milk, cinnamon, salt, and pepper. Spread over the top of ham. Top each piece of ham with a pineapple ring. Sprinkle top with the corn flakes. Bake uncovered, at 375° for 30 minutes.

SAUSAGE STUFFED SHELLS

½ 12 oz. pkg. jumbo pasta shells, cooked
3 hot or sweet sausages, casings removed
1 medium onion, diced
8 oz. pkg. fresh mushrooms, diced
1 cup part-skim ricotta
1 large egg
1 tsp. kosher salt, divided
1¾ cups Italian blend cheeses, shredded, divided
1 cup (2 oz.) baby spinach leaves
12 oz. eggplant, cut into ½" pieces
1 26 oz. jar garden style pasta sauce

MAKES 8 SERVINGS

Cook sausage in a large skillet, chopping into bits, remove and drain on paper towel; set aside. In same skillet, sauté onion and mushroom until onion is tender, about 8 to 10 minutes; set aside.

In a large bowl combine ricotta, egg, ¼ teaspoon salt, ½ cup cheese, and spinach. Add in cooked sausage and onion mixture into cheese mixture; set aside.

In the same skillet, cook eggplant stirring until just softened, about 8 minutes. Add pasta sauce and remaining salt; bring to a boil. Pour ⅔ of the eggplant sauce into a 2 quart casserole dish. Fill each shell with about 2 tablespoons of sausage mixture (wrap and freeze at this point if desired), arrange in dish and spoon remaining sauce over shells.

Cover and bake in 375° oven until sauce is bubbly, about 25 minutes. Remove from oven, sprinkle top with remaining cheese and bake uncovered, for 8 to 10 minutes or until cheese is melted.

PREP TIME: 30 MINUTES   COOK: 5 MINUTES
OVEN: 375°   BAKE: 20 MINUTES

1 14.5 oz. can whole tomatoes
2 cups water
1 pkg. Spanish rice mix
¼ cup butter, divided
1 T fresh lemon juice
12 thin slices boiled ham (1¼ lb.)
2 T flour
½ tsp. kosher salt
⅛ tsp. black pepper
1½ cups milk
1 cup cheddar cheese, finely shredded
1 T parsley, chopped

RICE-FILLED HAM POCKETS

MAKES 6 SERVINGS

Prepare the Spanish rice with the tomatoes, water, and butter per the package instructions adding the lemon juice to the mixture. Put about ⅓ cup of rice onto the center of each ham slice. Fold edges to the center to form a pocket. Place the pockets into a shallow 2 quart casserole.

Melt remaining butter in a small sauce pan. Blend in flour, salt, and pepper. Gradually stir in milk, stirring constantly and cook over low heat until thickened and smooth. Stir in grated cheese and parsley. Pour mixture over ham. Bake at 375° until hot and bubbly, about 20 minutes. If desired, brown lightly for 2 minutes under broiler.

TIP: *Most Spanish rice mixes call for tomatoes, water, and optional butter listed above. Check the package instructions and adjust accordingly.*

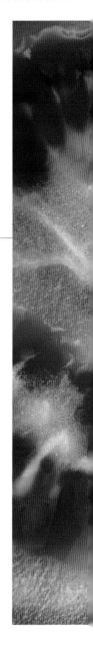

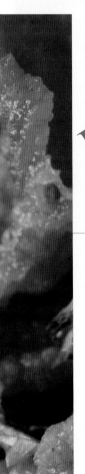

BACON & BLUE CHEESE TARTS

PREP TIME: 15 MINUTES   BAKE: 15-17 MINUTES

OVEN: 400°

6 slices bacon, roughly chopped

1 8.5 oz. pkg. corn muffin mix

⅔ cup all-purpose flour

1 tsp. chili powder

1 egg, slightly beaten

¼ cup milk

3 Granny Smith apples, cored, thinly sliced

⅓ cup blue cheese crumbles

fresh thyme (optional)

MAKES 4 SERVINGS

Cook bacon until crisp. Drain; reserve 1 tablespoon drippings. In a medium bowl, combine muffin mix, flour, chili powder, egg, and milk. Divide dough into 4 portions, place onto 2 greased baking sheets (2 portions per sheet) and press into 6 to 7 inch circles. Top each circle with a layer of apple slices, leaving a 1 inch border. Fold edges inward around apple slices. Brush apple slices and crust with reserved bacon drippings.

Bake in 400° oven for 10 minutes. Top tarts with bacon and blue cheese; bake 5 to 7 minutes more until edges are golden and bottom of crust is set. Sprinkle with thyme if desired.

CLEANING & DEVEINING SHRIMP

Shrimp that is peeled after cooking tends to retain more flavor but is also more difficult to peel and can be a bit messy. Shrimp peeled prior to cooking is easier to peel, allows the vein to be removed and will maintain a good presentation. Some seafood markets offer fresh shrimp that's already pre-cleaned. If you can't find it pre-cleaned, here's a basic way to clean and devein shrimp: If the head is still intact, lay on side and cut off head with a sharp knife. Hold the shrimp down on a cutting board by the legs or tail. With your other hand, insert the tip of a paring knife just below where the head was then carefully run the blade down the back of the shrimp stopping before reaching the tail. Use your fingers to peel off the shell and legs. Next, spread the cut line on the back open using your fingers and remove the vein. Now gently pull the tail off the shrimp.

CHAPTER TWELVE

CATCH OF THE DAY
FISH, SHELLFISH, & CRUSTACEANS

OVEN FRIED FISH

MAKES 4 SERVINGS

OVEN: 450°

1½ lbs. fish filets, salmon, trout or white fish
½ cup milk
½ cup flour
½ tsp. kosher salt
1 tsp. dried basil
1 tsp. chervil or dried dill
1 egg, beaten
½ cup fine dry bread crumbs
⅓ cup butter, melted, divided
fresh parsley & lemon wedges (optional)

Wash filets and pat dry. Cut into serving size pieces. Dip in milk then into a dry mixture of flour, salt, basil, and chervil. Add egg to the remaining milk. Add crumbs to the remaining flour mixture. Dip filets into egg-milk mixture then into flour-crumb mixture. Place filets into a buttered 2 quart baking dish and drizzle with remaining melted butter. Bake uncovered, at 450° for 10 to 15 minutes or until fish flakes with a fork. Garnish with parsley and lemon if desired.

TUNA & PEAS

MAKES 6 SERVINGS

PREP TIME: 10 MINUTES COOK: 5 MINUTES

OVEN: 375° BAKE: 20 MINUTES

1 10¾ oz. can condensed creamed soup
1¼ cup milk
¼ tsp. kosher salt
¼ tsp. black pepper
1⅓ cup minute rice
2 5 oz. cans tuna, drained
1 10 oz. box frozen peas, thawed
6 American cheese slices, quartered

Mix creamed soup, milk and salt. Bring to a boil stirring constantly. Layer rice, tuna, and peas in a lightly greased 2 quart casserole dish. Scatter the cheese over top. Top with soup mixture. Bake uncovered, at 375° for 20 minutes.

TIP: *This is great served with toast and topped with a little Tabasco hot pepper sauce.*

ROCKY MOUNTAIN TROUT

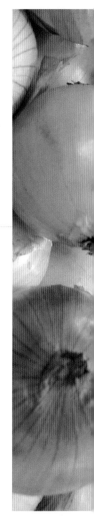

PREP TIME: 10 MINUTES COOK: 30 MINUTES

- ½ lb. bacon, roughly chopped
- 2 medium yellow onions, thinly sliced
- ⅓ cup yellow cornmeal
- ⅓ cup all-purpose flour
- 1 tsp. kosher salt
- ¼ tsp. ground black pepper
- 4 8 oz. trout filets, cleaned, scaled

MAKES 4 SERVINGS

Cook bacon in skillet until crisp; remove from skillet, drain on paper towels. Reserve 2 tablespoons of bacon drippings in skillet. Reserve the remaining drippings. Add sliced onions into skillet, breaking apart into rings; cook 10 minutes or until soft and begins to caramelize. Remove from skillet; set aside.

In a shallow dish, combine corn meal, flour, salt, and pepper. Coat trout filets thoroughly on both sides. Add 2 to 3 tablespoons of reserved bacon drippings into skillet. Pan-fry filets 6 to 8 minutes, turning once, until coating is crisp and fish flakes. Serve with onions and crumbled bacon around sides of filets.

Fresh!

POACHED SALMON WITH DILL SAUCE

1 cup plain low-fat yogurt
1 T fresh lemon juice
¼ cup fresh dill, chopped
2 cups low salt chicken broth
1 onion, sliced
1 celery stalk, sliced
kosher salt & black pepper to taste
4 salmon steaks, cut 1" thick

MAKES 4 SERVINGS

Blend yogurt, lemon juice, and dill in a small bowl. Lightly season with salt and pepper; set aside.

In a large skillet, combine chicken broth, onion, and celery. Bring to a boil over medium-high heat and cook for 2 minutes. Season both sides of salmon steaks with salt and pepper.

Add salmon into skillet with broth mixture; cover and reduce heat to a simmer. Poach until fish just starts to flake when prodded with a fork, 8 to 10 minutes. Serve steaks with a dollop of dill sauce.

Just a dollop!

3 T unsalted butter, melted, divided
¾ cup panko bread crumbs
1 lemon, zest & juice
3 T fresh dill, coarsely chopped
2 lbs. assorted potatoes, sliced
¾ tsp. kosher salt
½ tsp. ground pepper
4 oz. feta cheese, crumbled
¾ cup low-sodium chicken broth
1¼ lb. skinless salmon filet, 1" thick

POTATO SALMON BAKE

MAKES 6 SERVINGS

Combine 1 tablespoon butter, panko, lemon zest, and dill; set aside. Coat the bottom of a 2 quart casserole with 1 tablespoon of butter. Place half of the potatoes in bottom, season with salt and pepper and sprinkle with half of the feta. Repeat layers. Combine 1 tablespoon of butter and broth; pour over potatoes.

Cover and bake at 375° until potatoes are just softened, about 45 minutes. Remove potatoes from oven; set aside.

Cut salmon into 2 to 3 inch pieces and toss with lemon juice; sprinkle with ¼ teaspoon of salt. Place salmon over potatoes and sprinkle with panko crumb mixture. Increase oven temperature to 425° and bake uncovered, 12 to 15 minutes or until salmon is cooked through and crumbs are golden.

TIP: *Tossing fish with lemon juice enhances the flavor of the fish and also helps maintain a good color.*

CREAMED SALMON ON TOAST

- 3 T butter
- 3 T all-purpose flour
- 1 cup cold milk
- 1 10 oz. can baby peas, drained, liquid reserved
- 1 14.75 oz. can salmon, drained, picked through & flaked
- kosher salt & black pepper to taste
- 4 pieces of bread, toasted, cubed

MAKES 4 SERVINGS

In a medium sauce pan or skillet, melt butter over medium heat. Whisk in flour, stirring constantly until a smooth paste is formed. Gradually add in milk and the reserved liquid from peas, stirring constantly until a smooth thick gravy is reached.

Fold in salmon and peas, avoiding mashing the peas. Cook until heated through. Season salmon mixture with salt and pepper to taste. Serve over toasted bread cubes.

TIP: *This is one of my all-time favorite recipes that bring back fond memories of my Mom's cooking. I don't know if she made this dish so often because it was easy or because it was cheap to make. The presentation is not much to look at but it's a delicious comfort food that will have you asking for seconds.*

PREP TIME: BAKE:
15 MINUTES   8 MINUTES
OVEN: 450° COOK: 8-12 MINUTES

⅓ cup extra virgin olive oil
Zest & juice of 1 lemon
½ tsp. freshly ground black
    pepper
¼ tsp. kosher salt
12 oz. asparagus, trimmed
4 4 oz. tuna steaks, cut
    1" thick
1 5 oz. bag mixed greens
⅓ cup freshly shaved
    Parmesan cheese

TUNA PARMESAN

MAKES 4 SERVINGS

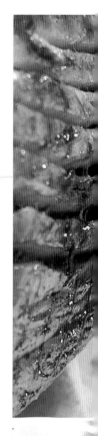

Make dressing by whisking together oil, lemon zest, lemon juice, pepper, and salt; set aside. Lay asparagus in single layer on a shallow baking pan. Drizzle with 2 tablespoons of dressing. Bake uncovered, at 450° for 8 minutes. Meanwhile, heat 1 tablespoon of dressing in a skillet over medium-high heat. Add tuna; cook 4 to 6 minutes each side, until browned and center is slightly pink. Divide the greens among 4 plates. Top with tuna and asparagus. Drizzle with remaining dressing and sprinkle with Parmesan.

PREP TIME: COOK:
15 MINUTES   1¾ HOUR

½ cup olive oil
1 dried red chili pepper,
    diced
1 large sweet onion,
    chopped
3 large garlic cloves, minced
    or mashed
½ cup fresh basil, chopped
    or 1 T dried
1 T oregano
kosher salt & black pepper
    to taste
2 4.5 oz. cans clams, drain,
    reserve liquid
1 lb. spaghetti, cooked per
    package directions
1 cup fresh parsley, chopped
3 T Parmesan cheese,
    grated + garnishing to
    taste
1 2 oz. jar pimento,
    chopped (optional)

CLAM SPAGHETTI

MAKES 6 SERVINGS

Heat olive oil slowly over low heat in a 2 quart sauce pan. Add chili pepper, onion, and garlic. Cook slowly over low heat for 30 minutes or until the onions are very soft. Add basil, oregano, salt, pepper, and reserved clam liquid. Continue to simmer for about 1 hour or until liquid is reduced down by half. Add clams, parsley, and 3 tablespoons of Parmesan cheese; continue to simmer at low for 15 minutes. Add pimento, if desired. Stir in cooked pasta and toss. Sprinkle generously with additional Parmesan cheese just before serving.

BROILED SHRIMP SCAMPI

MAKES 4 SERVINGS

PREP TIME:
10 MINUTES

BROIL:
10 MINUTES

1 lb. large shrimp, peeled, deveined
2 Roma tomatoes, peeled, seeded, chopped
¼ cup extra virgin olive oil
3 T red wine vinegar
1 T fresh basil or 1 tsp. dried basil
1 T fresh oregano or 1 tsp. dried oregano
1 garlic clove, minced
½ tsp. seasoning salt
½ tsp. hot pepper sauce
2 3 T dried bread crumbs

Place shrimp and tomatoes in an 8"x 11½"baking dish; set aside. Whisk together oil, vinegar, basil, oregano, garlic, seasoning salt, and hot sauce. Pour over shrimp and tomatoes, tossing gently to coat.

Broil 4 inches below broiler for 8 minutes stirring occasionally. Sprinkle with bread crumbs and broil another 2 minutes or until crumbs are lightly browned and shrimp is pink, not translucent.

EASY WAY TO PEEL TOMATOES

1. In a large pot, boil enough water to cover tomatoes.
2. Clean tomatoes and twist the stems off.
3. Score an X on the bottom of the tomato with a paring knife.
4. Immerse the scored tomato into the boiling water for no more than 30 to 45 seconds.
5. Remove tomato from boiling water and immediately place into a bowl of ice water.
6. After the tomatoes cool, remove from bath. Peel away tomato skin with fingers or use a paring knife if necessary.

Think pink!

PREP TIME: COOK: 25-
15 MINUTES   30 MINUTES

- 1 T butter or margarine
- 1 medium onion, sliced
- 1 medium green pepper, julienned
- 1 cup celery, sliced diagonally
- 1 bay leaf, crumbled
- 1 14.5 oz. can stewed tomatoes
- ½ cup water
- ½ tsp. kosher salt
- ⅛ tsp. cayenne pepper
- ⅛ tsp. paprika
- 1 clove garlic, minced
- 1 T flour
- 1½ cups medium shrimp, cooked
- 2 cups white rice, cooked

SHRIMP CREOLE

MAKES 4 SERVINGS

Melt butter in a large, deep skillet. Add onion, green pepper, and celery. Cook until the onion is soft and green pepper is tender-crisp. Add bay leaf, tomatoes, water, salt, cayenne pepper, paprika, and garlic. Simmer covered, for 15 minutes.

Mix flour with 2 tablespoons of water to make a paste. Add into tomato mixture and continue to cook until thickened. Add shrimp, stirring until warm. Taste and season with more salt if desired. Serve over rice.

PREP TIME:  COOK: 8-10
15 MINUTES   MINUTES

- 3 T all-purpose flour
- 1 tsp. lemon pepper
- 1 lb. large shrimp, cleaned, deveined
- 2 T olive oil
- 2 cloves garlic, minced
- ½ cup dry white wine
- ½ cup vegetable broth
- 3 T fresh lemon juice
- 2 T capers
- 2 T unsalted butter
- 1 T fresh parsley, chopped
- 2 cups white rice, cooked

SHRIMP PICCATA

MAKES 4 SERVINGS

Combine flour and pepper in a shallow dish or sealable plastic bag. Toss shrimp in flour mixture until well coated. In a medium skillet, heat oil over medium-high heat. Add shrimp and cook for 2 minutes; turn cook another minute. Cook in batches if necessary. Remove shrimp to a plate; set aside.

Add garlic to skillet and cook 1 minute. Stir in wine, broth, lemon juice, and capers. Bring to a simmer. Add shrimp and cook 1 minute, until heated through. Remove from heat; stir in butter and parsley. Serve over rice.

CHILI BUTTERED SHRIMP

PREP TIME:
15 MINUTES

COOK:
15 MINUTES

3 T unsalted butter, divided
1½ cups onion, finely chopped
1 lb. raw shrimp, peeled, deveined
2 tsp. dark chili powder
2 T fresh lime juice
½ tsp. kosher salt
¼ tsp. black pepper
lime wedges (optional)

MAKES 4 SERVINGS

Melt 1 tablespoon butter in a skillet. Add onion and cook 7 minutes or until beginning to brown on edges, stirring frequently. Add shrimp, cook for 2 minutes. Add chili powder and cook 2 more minutes or until shrimp is opaque in center; remove from heat. Stir in lime juice, salt, and pepper. Cover and let stand for 3 minutes. Serve with lime wedges if desired.

HERBED CRAB CAKES

PREP TIME:
20 MINUTES

COOK:
6 MINUTES

SET: 10 MINUTES   CHILL: 1 HOUR

⅔ cup mayonnaise
2 T green onions, minced
1 large egg yolk
1 T fresh lemon juice
½ tsp. lemon zest
2 tsp. fresh dill, minced
2 tsp. fresh tarragon, minced
2 tsp. fresh cilantro, minced
1 tsp. Dijon mustard
⅛ tsp. black pepper
8 oz. blue crabmeat, picked through
1½ cups Panko bread crumbs, divided
2 T butter
2 T grape seed or olive oil

MAKES 4 SERVINGS

In a large bowl, whisk together the first 10 ingredients. Fold in crabmeat and ½ cup panko crumbs, breaking up crabmeat slightly; let stand 10 minutes. Line a baking sheet with wax paper and spread remaining panko crumbs on sheet. Form crab mixture into 8 two inch diameter patties using about ¼ cup for each. Press both sides into panko crumbs. Cover and put in refrigerator for at least 1 hour, but no longer than 1 day. In a large skillet, heat butter and oil. Cook crab cakes 3 minutes on each side, adding more butter and oil as needed.

PREP TIME: COOK:
10 MINUTES   *10 MINUTES*
OVEN: *400°*   BAKE: *10 MINUTES*

- ½ cup unsalted butter (1 stick)
- 8 oz. fresh mushrooms, sliced
- ¼ cup flour
- 1 tsp. kosher salt
- ½ tsp. dry mustard
- 2 cups milk
- ¾ lb. large shrimp, cooked, deveined
- ½ cup parmesan cheese, shredded
- dash paprika

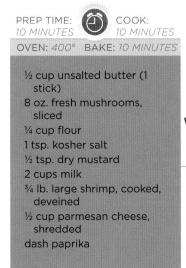

SHRIMP THERMIDOR

MAKES 8 SERVINGS

Melt butter and sauté mushrooms until softened. Add in flour, salt, and dry mustard; stir to form a paste. Slowly add milk stirring constantly until the mixture thickens. Coarsely chop shrimp then add into sauce; mix well.

Place shrimp mixture into individual baking dishes. Sprinkle with cheese and paprika. Bake at 400° for 10 minutes.

SELECTING & HANDLING FRESH SHRIMP

Here are a few basic things to look for when you buy fresh shrimp:
• First, give it a smell test. It should smell like the sea or seaweed. If it has a strong ammonia odor or smells like an old fish, don't buy it.
• You may want to give it the touch test as well. Fresh shrimp will be wet not slimy and have a firm, slightly translucent body.
• Finally, always remember to rinse fresh shrimp well with cold water to remove any residual film left over from the seafood market.

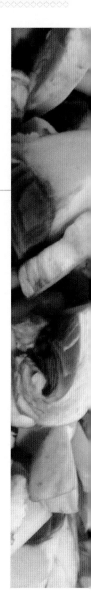

CHAPTER THIRTEEN

VEGETARIAN SELECTIONS
MAIN-DISH MEALS

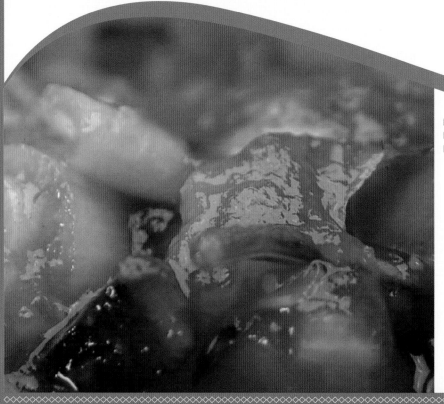

MEXICAN LASAGNA
ROASTED VEGETABLE PIE
BLACK BEAN TACOS

PREP TIME: *15 MINUTES* **COOK:** *3½ HOURS*
SLOW COOK: *HIGH*

1 head cauliflower
3 plum tomatoes, seeds removed, chopped
1 15.5 oz. can black beans, drained, rinsed
3½ cups Monterey Jack cheese, shredded
1 cup frozen corn
⅓ cup fresh cilantro, chopped
2 tsp. chili powder
2 tsp. ground cumin
1 16 oz. jar tomatillo salsa
6 large flour tortillas
sour cream (optional)

MEXICAN LASAGNA

MAKES 8 SERVINGS

Cut cauliflower into flowerets then slice into ½ inch slices (about 6 cups). Place cauliflower, tomatoes, beans, corn, and cilantro in a large bowl. Sprinkle with chili powder and cumin and stir to combine.

Lightly grease or coat the inside of a slow cooker with a non-stick cooking spray. Spread about ⅓ of cauliflower mixture in bottom of cooker, sprinkle ⅓ cup cheese, spread ⅓ of salsa, and place 2 tortillas on top. Repeat layering 2 more times, setting aside the last 2 tortillas. Cut these tortillas into 2 inch pieces and scatter over top.

Cook on high for 3 hours or low for 5½ hours or until cauliflower is tender. Top with the remaining cheese, cover and cook for 30 additional minutes or until cheese has melted. Let sit 10 minutes. Serve with sour cream and remaining salsa if desired.

PREP TIME:
15 MINUTES

COOK:
90 MINUTES

OVEN: 450°/425°

ROASTED VEGETABLE PIE

MAKES 6 SERVINGS

Toss first 5 ingredients together with oil and ¼ teaspoon each of salt and pepper. Spread out on lightly greased jelly roll pan. Bake at 450° for 30 minutes stirring halfway.

Combine broth and cornstarch in a saucepan. Bring to a boil, lower heat and simmer 1 minute, stirring constantly until thickened. Add thyme, oregano and remaining salt and pepper. In a large bowl, gently toss roasted vegetables, sauce, and crumbs.

Fit 1 pie crust into a lightly greased 9 inch pie plate. Sprinkle 1 tablespoon of cheese over the bottom. Spoon vegetable mixture into crust; sprinkle with remaining cheese. Place the remaining pie crust on top and crimp crusts together. Cut slits with a knife to vent. Brush lightly with the egg-water mixture. Bake at 450° for 15 minutes, lower heat to 425° and bake for 30 more minutes. Allow to cool slightly before slicing.

- ½ small cauliflower (4 cups), cut small into flowerets
- ½ small butternut squash, peeled, ½" cubes
- 2 medium parsnips, peeled, cut into ½" cubes
- 1 cup baby carrots, sliced into ½" coins
- 1 sweet red pepper, cut into 1" pieces
- 2 T olive oil
- ½ tsp. kosher salt, divided
- ½ tsp. black pepper, divided
- 1 cup vegetable broth
- 1 T cornstarch
- ¾ tsp. dried thyme
- ¾ tsp. dried oregano
- 2 T plain bread crumbs
- 1 15 oz. pkg. rolled pie crusts
- 2 T Parmesan cheese, grated, divided
- 1 egg + 1 T water, beaten

PREP TIME:  COOK:
10 MINUTES   5 MINUTES

1 15 oz. can black beans
1 tsp. ground cumin
kosher salt & black pepper
  to taste
5 tsp. olive oil, divided
2 cups shredded cabbage
2 green onions, thinly sliced
⅓ cup fresh cilantro,
  chopped
4 white or yellow corn
  tortillas
⅓ cup feta cheese,
  crumbled
hot sauce to taste
  (optional)

BLACK BEAN TACOS

MAKES 4 SERVINGS

Place beans, cumin, salt, and pepper in a small bowl and partially mash; set aside. In a medium bowl, combine 2 teaspoons olive oil with lime juice. Add cabbage, green onions, and cilantro; toss to coat; set aside.

Heat remaining olive oil in a large non-stick skillet over medium-high heat. Add tortillas in single layer and spoon ¼ of bean mixture onto one half of each tortilla; cook 1 minute. Fold tacos in half; cook until golden brown, about 1 minute each side. Fill tacos with cabbage mixture and top with feta cheese. Add hot sauce if desired.

CLEARING THE AIR

Black beans are an excellent source of protein and fiber (soluble and insoluble) that help promote good digestive health, lowers cholesterol, stabilizes blood sugar (energy level), and provides optimal protection against cancer.

If you are not eating beans because you're worried it will cause a "gassy" concern, start by eating small portions and increase your fiber intake gradually. Your body will adjust to consistent fiber intake and you will be less "windy" in no time. —101 foods

CHAPTER FOURTEEN

HAPPY ENDINGS
DESSERTS & COOKIES

1 cup flour
1½ cups powdered sugar
1½ cups egg whites (about 12), room temperature
1½ tsp. cream of tartar
1 cup granulated sugar
¼ tsp. salt
1½ tsp. vanilla
½ tsp. almond extract

MAKES 6-8 SERVINGS

Preheat oven to 375°. Mix flour and powdered sugar; set aside. Beat egg whites and cream of tartar in a large mixing bowl on medium speed until foamy. Beat in granulated sugar on high speed, 2 tablespoons at a time. Continue beating until stiff and glossy. Add salt, vanilla, and almond extract with the last addition of sugar. Do not under beat. Sprinkle the flour and sugar mixture, ¼ cup at a time over the meringue, folding in just until the mixture blends.

Push batter into an ungreased 10" x 4" tube pan. Cut gently through batter with a metal spatula. Bake until cracks feel dry and top springs back when touched lightly, about 30 to 35 minutes. Invert pan on funnel, let hang until cake is cold. Remove from pan.

BEATING EGG WHITES

1. Let the eggs sit out for at least 30 minutes to bring them to room temperature. It will help to get more volume.

2. Use a deep bowl with a rounded bottom. A copper bowl is ideal because it reacts chemically with the egg whites to help form fluffy, high peaks. If you don't have a copper bowl, use a stainless steel bowl and add a little cream of tartar or fresh lemon juice to achieve the same result.

3. Start at a slow speed and work your way up to high. Stop when your egg whites get fluffy. Over beating will cause them to liquefy again.

COCONUT CREAM CAKE

PREP TIME: *15 MINUTES*   BAKE: *15 MINUTES*

OVEN: *350°* FREEZE: *15 MINUTES*

1 3.5 oz. can flaked coconut
1 angel food cake, day old
¼ cup seedless raspberry jam
½ pint raspberry sherbet
1 cup heavy cream

MAKES 6-8 SERVINGS

Preheat oven to 350°. Spread coconut in a single layer of a baking sheet. Bake for 15 minutes stirring occasionally; set aside to cool.

With a long serrated knife, cut 1-inch layer from top of cake. With a sharp knife cut 2 circles around inside of cake 1 inch apart and 1½ inch deep. Gently pull out cake between the circles.

Spread 2 tablespoons jam on bottom and sides of tunnel. Fill with scoops of sherbet. Spoon the remaining jam over sherbet. Replace top, cover and freeze cake for 15 minutes.

Meanwhile, beat cream until stiff peaks form. Frost the cake, press coconut onto sides and top. Cover and place back into freezer until ready to serve.

TIP: *It is best to let the cake sit for a few minutes after removing it from the freezer before serving.*

Going coconuts!

PREP TIME: CHILL:
30 MINUTES *2-4 HOURS*

- 1 large angel food cake
- 1 cup butter, softened
- 1½ cups superfine sugar, sifted
- pinch of salt
- 2 egg yolks, whites reserved
- 1 tsp. vanilla
- 6 T double strength coffee, cold
- 2 squares un-sweet chocolate, melted
- ½ pint whipping cream
- 1 – 21 oz. can cherries (optional)

MOCHA TORTE

MAKES 10 SERVINGS

Slice cake horizontally into 5 slices; set aside. Cream the butter and sugar together. Add salt, vanilla, and egg yolks beating thoroughly. Add coffee and chocolate; beat until well combined. Beat the egg whites until stiff then fold into mocha mixture. Spread mixture between layers and on outside of cake. Cover and chill in refrigerator for 2 to 4 hours or until icing is firm. Whip cream and top and sides of frosted cake 1 hour before serving; re-chill. Slice and top with cherries if desired.

PREP TIME:  BAKE: *50-*
15 MINUTES *60 MINUTES*

OVEN: *350°*

- 1¾ cups sugar, divided
- 1 11 oz. box NILLA wafers, crushed, divided
- ½ cup pecans, chopped
- 1 tsp. ground cinnamon
- ¼ cup butter, softened
- 6 eggs
- 1 8 oz. container sour cream
- 2 tsp. baking powder
- ½ tsp. baking soda
- ¼ tsp. salt

SOUR CREAM COFFEE CAKE

MAKES 6 SERVINGS

Combine ½ cup sugar, ½ cup wafer crumbs, pecans, and cinnamon in a bowl; set aside. Combine the remaining sugar and butter in a mixing bowl and beat on high speed until light and fluffy. Add eggs and sour cream, continuing to beat. Stir in remaining wafer crumbs, baking powder, baking soda, and salt. Pour half of the batter into a bundt pan that is lightly greased and floured. Sprinkle with half of the nut mix; swirl with a spatula. Pour remaining batter; top with remaining cinnamon and swirl. Bake at 350° for 50 to 60 minutes. Cool 10 minutes in pan; transfer to wire rack to cool.

PENNSYLVANIA DUTCH SHOO-FLY CAKE

PREP TIME: 15 MINUTES

BAKE: *45-50 MINUTES*

OVEN: *350°*

4 cups flour
2 cups sugar
1 cup butter, softened
1 tsp. cinnamon
1 cup Grandma's Molasses (gold Label)
2 cups boiling water
2 tsp. baking soda
whipped cream (optional)

MAKES 10-12 SERVINGS

In a large mixing bowl, combine flour, sugar, butter, and cinnamon. Remove and reserve 1½ cups of dry mixture for cake topping. Place molasses in a 4 cup Pyrex measuring pitcher. Add water and baking soda, stir well. Combine molasses mixture with dry ingredient mixture, stirring well until smooth.

Pour into a greased and floured 9" x 13" baking pan. Top with reserved dry ingredient mixture. Bake at 350° for 45 to 50 minutes or until toothpick comes out clean.

TIP: *Shoo-fly cake is best served warm and with whipped cream on top.*

SHOO-FLY DON'T BOTHER ME

This well-known nursery rhyme, first published in 1869, has remained a popular tune over the many decades. It's now a popular song for children but the original lyrics were very offensive, at least by today's standards, and not so child-friendly. If you are curious about the original lyrics, you can find them on Wikipedia.

The original version gained in popularity during the Spanish-American War and was commonly sung by the soldiers when the flies and the yellow fever mosquitos were a serious enemy.

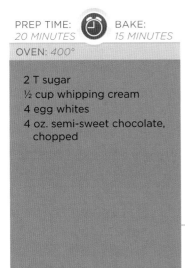

PREP TIME: 20 MINUTES
BAKE: 15 MINUTES
OVEN: 400°

2 T sugar
½ cup whipping cream
4 egg whites
4 oz. semi-sweet chocolate, chopped

SO-EASY CHOCOLATE SOUFFLÉ

MAKES 4 SERVINGS

Preheat oven to 400°. Coat insides of ramekins with a non-stick cooking spray, sprinkle with sugar and place on a baking sheet; set aside. Combine chocolate and cream in a micro-safe bowl and microwave on high for 1½ to 2 minutes until smooth, stirring twice. Divide in half. Cover and cool to room temperature. In a large mixing bowl, beat egg whites until foamy. Gradually add sugar, beating until soft peaks form. Gently fold half of the cooled chocolate mixture into the beaten egg whites until combined.

Spoon the chocolate mixture into 4 ramekins. Bake for 12 to 15 minutes or until knife comes out clean. To serve, use a spoon or knife to split open to centers of the soufflés; pour in remaining chocolate mixture. Serve immediately.

TIPS FOR THE PERFECT SOUFFLÉ

Soufflés are easy to make but are temperamental. They don't like interruptions, so before you get started, make sure you have read the recipe, the ingredients are weighed or measured, the mixing equipment is oil-free and clean, and the ramekins are greased. All ingredients, especially the eggs, should be at room temperature. Preheat the oven so the soufflé can go directly in when ready. Try to not open the oven door while cooking. A sudden change in temperature can cause the soufflé to drop.
Soufflés are best served fresh out of the oven.

BUTTERCREAM FROSTING

PREP TIME:
10 MINUTES

½ cup butter, softened
⅛ tsp. salt
3½ cups confectioners' sugar, sifted, divided
¼ cup milk
1 tsp. vanilla

MAKES 2 CUPS

Cream the butter, salt, and 1 cup of confectioners' sugar together until light and fluffy. Add remaining sugar, milk, and vanilla. Beat until very smooth.

TIP: *For stiffer frosting, reduce milk and increase sugar.*

CHOCOLATE FROSTING

PREP TIME: 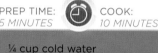 COOK:
5 MINUTES   10 MINUTES

¼ cup cold water
4 T cocoa
1 cup superfine sugar
3 T corn starch
pinch of salt
¾ cup boiling hot water
3 T butter
1 tsp. vanilla

MAKES 2 CUPS

Combine cold water, cocoa, sugar, corn starch, and salt in a small sauce pan, mixing well. Add boiling water and cook over medium heat, stirring steadily until mixture is thick. Add butter and vanilla. Mix well. Cool before spreading.

DUMP CAKE

1 20 oz. can crushed pineapple, drained
1 21 oz. can cherry pie filling
1 16.5 oz. box white cake mix
½ cup butter (1 stick)

MAKES 6-8 SERVINGS

Pour in crushed pineapple into a greased 9" x 13" baking pan. Top with cherry pie filling spreading out evenly in dish. Sprinkle cake mix on top. Dot the top with slices of butter. Bake at 350° for about 45 minutes or until golden brown.

ÉCLAIR CAKE

2 3 oz. pkgs. vanilla instant pudding
1 8 oz. tub frozen whipped topping, thawed
1 14.4 oz. box graham crackers
1 12 oz. tub chocolate frosting

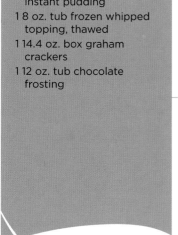

MAKES 12 SERVINGS

Prepare pudding per package instructions; set aside. Line a 9" x 13" cake pan with whole graham crackers filling in all the spaces.

Fold whipped topping into pudding. Pour half of pudding over crackers. Top with a layer of crackers, then the remaining pudding. Top with another layer of crackers, and spread with chocolate frosting. Refrigerate at least overnight.

Chocolate!

APPLE STRUDEL

PREP TIME: 10 MINUTES

BAKE: 40 MINUTES

OVEN: 375°

3½ cups Rice Chex cereal, lightly crushed
2 apples, peeled, sliced
½ cup light brown sugar
dash of nutmeg
½ tsp. cinnamon
2 T butter

MAKES 6 SERVINGS

Grease a 2 quart baking dish. Mix sugar, nutmeg, and cinnamon together. Arrange cereal crumbs and apples in layers, sprinkling apples with sugar mixture. Dot the top with butter. Cover and bake at 375° for about 40 minutes or until apples are soft.

CHOOSING THE BEST APPLE

Confused about which kind of apple to pick for your recipe or just a good one to snack on? The chart below gives you a quick reference on some of the apples commonly found in the supermarket.

VARIETY	SNACK	SALAD	BAKE	COOK	PIE	DRY	OTHER
Baldwin			X	X			Cider
Braeburn	X	X	X	X	X		Sauce
Fiji	X	X	X		X		Sauce
Gala	X	X	X		X	X	Sauce
Golden Delicious	X	X	X	X	X		Sauce
Granny Smith	X	X	X	X	X		
Honeycrisp	X	X	X	X	X	X	Sauce
Lady	X						Sauce
McIntosh	X	X	X	X			Sauce
Pink Lady	X	X	X		X		
Red Delicious	X	X					

BLUEBERRY CREAM TART

PREP TIME: 15 MINUTES • BAKE: 25-30 MINUTES
OVEN: 350° CHILL: 6 HOURS

- ¾ cups graham cracker crumbs (12 squares), crushed
- 6 T butter or margarine, softened
- ½ cup sugar
- 1 8 oz. pkg. cream cheese
- 1 tsp. lemon zest
- ½ tsp. pure vanilla extract
- 2 eggs
- 1 21 oz. can blueberry pie filling

MAKES 6 SERVINGS

Combine graham cracker crumbs, butter, and sugar together and press into the bottom of a greased 8" x 8" baking pan. Cream together the cream cheese and sugar. Add zest and vanilla; mix well. Beat in 1 egg at a time mixing well. Pour into crust and bake at 350° for 25 to 30 minutes. Cool and spread the blueberries on top. Cover and chill for 6 hours.

CHOCOLATE MARASCHINO CHERRIES

PREP TIME: 20 MINUTES • COOK: 5 MINUTES

- 1 4.4 oz. milk chocolate bar
- 1 T orange juice
- ½ cup unsalted almonds, chopped
- ½ cup unsalted cashews, chopped
- ¼ tsp. ground nutmeg
- 1 10 oz. jar maraschino cherries with stems

MAKES ABOUT 2 DOZEN

Melt chocolate bar with orange juice. Remove from heat; fold in nuts and nutmeg. Using your hands, mold the mixture around cherries in shape of a cone, letting stems hang out top. Store the cherries in a cool place.

CHERRY COCONUT NUT BARS

- 1¼ cup flour, divided
- 1 cup butter (2 sticks), softened, divided
- 2¼ cups powdered sugar, divided
- 2 eggs, beaten
- 1 cup sugar
- ½ tsp. baking powder
- ¼ tsp. salt
- ¾ cups walnuts, chopped
- ½ cup coconut
- ½ 14.5 oz. can cherries in water, drain reserving 2 T juice

MAKES 12-16 BARS

Combine 1 cup of flour, ½ cup butter, and ¼ cup of powdered sugar until smooth and creamy. Press into a 9" x 13" baking pan. Bake at 350° for 15 to 20 minutes until golden brown.

Beat together eggs, sugar, remaining flour, baking powder, and salt. Add walnuts, coconut, and cherries; mix well. Pour onto crust and bake for 25 minutes. Cool. Beat remaining butter, powdered sugar, and cherry juice until fluffy. Ice the top of baked filling and cut into square bars.

CHERRY CHEESECAKE

- 1 pkg. white cake mix
- 2 pkgs. cream cheese
- 4 cups confectioners' sugar
- 1 pint whipping cream, whipped
- 2 21 oz. cans cherry pie filling

MAKES 25-30 SERVINGS

Prepare cake mix per package instructions. Pour into 2 greased 9" x 13" baking pans. Bake at 350° for 20 minutes or until toothpick comes out clean. Cool.

In a mixing bowl, beat the cream cheese and sugar until fluffy. Fold in whipped cream. Spread over each cake. Top with pie filling. Chill for 4 hours or overnight.

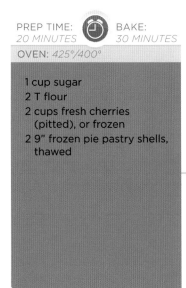

PREP TIME:
20 MINUTES

BAKE:
30 MINUTES

OVEN: 425°/400°

1 cup sugar
2 T flour
2 cups fresh cherries
(pitted), or frozen
2 9" frozen pie pastry shells,
thawed

CHERRY PIE

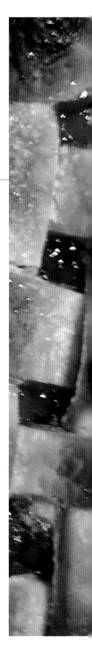

MAKES 1 PIE

Blend sugar, flour, and cherries. If you use frozen cherries, thaw and drain. Fit 1 pie pastry shell into a 9 inch pie plate. Pour in cherry mixture. Cover with remaining pie pastry and press edges firmly together. Cut slits on top to let out steam.

Bake for 10 minutes at 425°, reduce to 400° and continue to cook for 15 to 20 minutes or until nicely browned. Cool on a rack. Serve slightly warmed.

LIFE'S A BOWL OF CHERRIES

Cherries are a low calorie fruit that offer high levels of vitamins, minerals, nutrients, and are high in fiber. Many ongoing studies show that cherries contain anti–inflammatory compounds that help relieve the pain of arthritis, fibromyalgia, gout, headaches and sports injuries.

In addition, significant levels of melatonin, a chemical hormone secreted by the brain, are found in cherries. Melatonin helps regulate sleeping habits and produces a calming effect on the brain that may help calm nervous system irritability, insomnia, and headaches.

Top off your day with the recommended daily serving of 20 cherries and sleep well, my friend.

ANGEL PIE

MAKES 6-8 SERVINGS

PREP TIME: 20 MINUTES   COOK: 50-55 MINUTES

OVEN: 300°   CHILL: 2 HOURS

2 egg whites
⅛ tsp. salt
⅛ tsp. cream of tartar
½ cup sugar
½ cup finely chopped walnuts or pecans
1½ tsp. vanilla, divided
1¼ lb. pkg. Baker's German sweet chocolate
3 T water
1 cup whipping cream (½ pint)

Combine egg whites, salt, and cream of tartar in a medium bowl. Beat until foamy. Add sugar 2 tablespoons at a time, beating after each addition until sugar is blended. Continue to beat until mixture stands in very stiff peaks. Fold in nuts and ½ teaspoon of vanilla.

Spoon the mixture into a lightly greased 8" pie pan, making a nest-like shell. Build up the sides ½ inch above the sides of the pan. Bake at 300° for 50 to 55 minutes. Cool to room temperature.

Melt chocolate and water in a saucepan over low heat. Stirring constantly until chocolate has melted. Cool until thickened. Add vanilla. Whip the whipping cream and fold into chocolate mixture. Pile into meringue shell. Chill for 2 hours before serving.

PREP TIME:  BAKE: *25-30*
15 MINUTES *MINUTES*

OVEN: *425°*

- 3 eggs, slightly beaten
- ½ cup sugar
- ¼ tsp. salt
- ¼ tsp. nutmeg
- 2 cups milk + 2 T, scalded, divided
- 1 9" frozen pastry shell, thawed
- ½ cup semi-sweet chocolate morsels

CHOCOLATE TOPPED CUSTARD PIE

MAKES 6 SERVINGS

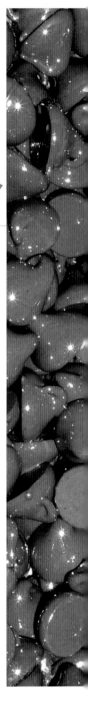

Combine eggs, sugar, salt, and nutmeg. Stir in 2 cups hot milk, mixing well. Pour into pastry shell. Bake at 425° for 25 to 30 minutes or until a knife comes out clean and there is a slight jiggle in the middle of the pie. Cool pie on rack.

Meanwhile, melt chocolate in double boiler or in microwave. Add remaining milk, stirring constantly until smooth and glossy. Spread chocolate mixture evenly on top of custard pie. Chill in refrigerator until serving.

CHOCOLATE UNWRAPPED

• *Chocolate is a natural anti-depressant, producing serotonin, a mood elevating chemical. So eat up and be happy!*

• *The chemical, phenylethylamine, also found in chocolate, is the same chemical the brain produces when you're in love.*

• *The popular belief that chocolate produces acne is a myth.*

• *Dark chocolate is rich in antioxidants which reduces the risk of cancer and heart disease.*

• *Chocolate is poisonous to dogs and other animals. It contains the chemical theobromine which is a stimulant and can cause seizures and even death.*

CHOCOLATE WHIPPED CREAM PIE

⅔ cup sugar
¼ cup cocoa
⅛ tsp. salt
1 cup milk
1 envelope unflavored gelatin
¼ cup cold water
1 cup heavy cream, whipped
½ tsp. vanilla
1 9" baked pie pastry or crumb shell

MAKES 1 PIE

Combine sugar, cocoa, and salt in a sauce pan. Stir in milk; heat to boiling. Remove from heat. Dissolve gelatin in cold water then add into the hot cocoa mixture. Chill until mixture begins to thicken, about 1 hour. Add whipped cream and vanilla to chocolate mixture and beat until fluffy and smooth.

Pour into pie shell and chill for 2 hours or until firm. Garnish with additional whipped cream if desired.

POTS DE CRÉME

¾ cup milk, less 2 T
1 cup Ghirardelli mini semi-sweet chocolate bits
1 egg
2 T sugar
1 tsp. vanilla
pinch of salt

MAKES 4 SERVINGS

Heat the milk to a boiling point, stirring constantly. Blend remaining ingredients thoroughly in a blender. Add in milk and blend for 1 minute. Pour into 4 pots de crème pots (ramekins) and chill until firm, about 4 to 6 hours.

TIP: *Just before serving, put a dollop of whipped cream on top and sprinkle with shaved chocolate.*

PREP TIME:
30 MINUTES

CHILL:
2 HOURS

- 1 cup sweet butter, softened
- 2 cups powder sugar
- 4 squares un-sweet chocolate, melted
- 4 eggs, beat until fluffy
- ¾ tsp. mint, rum, or almond flavoring
- 2 tsp. vanilla
- ½ 11 oz. box vanilla wafers, crushed (about 24 wafers)

FRANGOS

MAKES 18 SERVINGS

Cream together butter, sugar, and eggs, beating until smooth. Mix melted chocolate with vanilla and flavoring. Combine chocolate and butter mixtures together, beating until smooth and creamy.

Place 1 tablespoon of vanilla wafer crumbs in the bottom of cupcake liners or ramekins. Spoon the chocolate mixture into each liner or ramekin, filling about ⅔ full. Sprinkle tops with more wafer crumbs. Refrigerate until set, about 2 hours.

WHAT IS A FRANGO?

Frangos are chocolate truffles offered traditionally in a mint, almond, orange, and maple flavors. They were first developed in 1918 for the Frederick and Nelson department stores in Seattle. It was later acquired, refined and widely popularized by the Marshall Field's department stores. Today, Frangos are now produced and distributed by Macy's department stores.

There are numerous theories on how they arrived with the name Frango. *One theory is that it's an acronym for* **FR***ederick* **A***nd* **N***elson* **GO***odness. The name and recipe has taken many turns since the original version. I think you'll find the recipe above is a delicious homemade interpretation of this infamous treat.*

Truffles!

BAKLAVA

MAKES 3 DOZEN

PREP TIME: 20 MINUTES
BAKE: 45 MINUTES
OVEN: 350°   SET: 24 HOURS

1 17¼ oz. pkg. phyllo pastry, thawed
1¼ cups butter, melted
1¼ cups flaked coconut, lightly toasted
½ cup macadamia nuts, finely chopped
½ cup pecans, finely chopped
½ cup brown sugar, firmly packed
1 tsp. ground allspice
1 cup sugar
½ cup water
¼ cup honey

Butter a 9" x 13" x 2" baking pan. Cover phyllo with a damp towel to keep moist. Cut 1 sheet of phyllo in half crosswise, and cut 1 half to fit into pan; brush with butter. Layer 10 sheets, brushing each sheet with butter.

Combine coconut, macadamia nuts, pecans, brown sugar, and allspice; stir well. Sprinkle ⅓ of mixture over layered phyllo sheets in pan. Layer 10 more phyllo sheets, brushing each sheet with butter. Repeat procedure twice with remaining nuts mixture, phyllo, and butter, ending with buttered phyllo.

Cut diagonally into diamond shapes using a sharp knife. Bake baklava at 350° for 45 minutes or until top is browned. Let cool completely.

Combine 1 cup sugar, water, and honey in a medium saucepan. Bring to a boil; reduce heat and simmer 5 minutes. Remove from heat; drizzle syrup over baklava. Cover and let stand at room temperature 24 hours.

PREP TIME: 20 MINUTES BAKE: 40 MINUTES
OVEN: *350°*

½ lb. fresh cranberries
1 cup sugar, divided
¼ cup water
1 orange, juice & grated peel
⅔ cup unsalted butter, softened
2 eggs
1½ cup flour
1½ tsp. baking powder
½ cup milk
2 T sour cream
2 T fresh nutmeg or to taste

CRANBERRY KUCHEN

MAKES 6-8 SERVINGS

Lightly grease and flour an 8 inch round baking pan; set aside. In a small saucepan, combine cranberries, ½ cup sugar, water, and orange juice. Bring to a boil, reduce heat and cook until the cranberries are soft, about 10 minutes; set aside.

In a mixing bowl, cream the butter and ½ cup sugar until smooth. Add 1 egg at a time stirring well to incorporate. Sift the flour and baking powder then stir in flour, milk, and sour cream into butter mixture alternating each a little at a time. Add nutmeg and orange rind, mixing well. Pour batter into prepared pan and top with the cranberry mixture. Bake at 350° for 40 minutes or until golden brown.

PREP TIME: 20 MINUTES CHILL: 1 HOUR

1 6 oz. pkg. semi-sweet chocolate morsels
¼ cup corn syrup
1 T butter
1 T water
2 cups corn flakes

CANDY COOKIES

MAKES 2 DOZEN

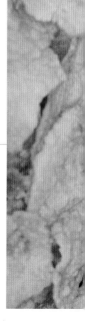

Combine chocolate chips with corn syrup, butter, and water in a medium saucepan stirring constantly until melted and heated thoroughly. Cover and simmer on low heat for 8 minutes. Remove from heat and stir in corn flakes. Drop by teaspoons on a waxed paper lined cookie sheet and chill until set about 1 hour.

EASY PUMPKIN PIE

PREP TIME: *10 MINUTES*   COOK: *5 MINUTES*

CHILL: *3 HOURS*

- 1 3 oz. pkg. cook & serve vanilla pudding & pie filling
- ¼ cup brown sugar, firmly packed
- ¾ tsp. ground cinnamon
- ½ tsp. ground nutmeg
- ¼ tsp. ground ginger
- ¼ tsp. salt
- 1¼ cup milk
- 1 T butter
- 1 15 oz. can pumpkin or 1¾ cup fresh, cooked, mashed
- 1 9" pie pastry shell, baked, cooled

MAKES 1 PIE

Combine pie filling mix, sugar, cinnamon, nutmeg, ginger, salt, milk, and butter in saucepan. Cook and stir over medium heat until mixture comes to a full boil. Remove from heat and cool for 5 minutes stirring once or twice. Add pumpkin, stirring until well blended. Pour into prepared pie shell and chill for 3 hours or until firm. Garnish with whipped cream.

MOLASSES COOKIES

PREP TIME: *30 MINUTES*   BAKE: *10-12 MINUTES*

OVEN: *375°*

- 1¼ cup sugar, divided
- 1 cup shortening
- 1 egg
- 1 tsp. salt
- 1 tsp. ground ginger
- 1 tsp. ground cinnamon
- 1 cup molasses
- 1 cup cold water
- 3 tsp. baking soda
- 1 rounded tsp. baking powder
- 4 to 6 cups flour

MAKES 5-6 DOZEN

Cream together 1 cup sugar, shortening, egg, ginger, cinnamon, and molasses. Combine water with baking soda and baking powder. Add to sugar mixture combining thoroughly. Add flour gradually until the dough is slightly thicker than for drop cookies.

Chill dough for about 30 minutes. Roll 1" dough balls between your hands. Place on a greased cookie sheet and press flat to about ¼" thick. Sprinkle sugar on top then lightly pat or roll surface to press sugar in. Bake at 375° for 10 to 12 minutes.

PREP TIME: 20 MINUTES  BAKE: 25-30 MINUTES

OVEN: 400°

6 T sugar
4 cups rhubarb, trimmed, cut into ½" pieces
1½ tsp. cornstarch
¼ cup uncooked rolled oats
¼ cup light brown sugar, packed
3 T all-purpose flour
¼ tsp. cinnamon
3 T unsalted butter, chilled, cut into pieces

RHUBARB CRISPS

MAKES 6 SERVINGS

Combine sugar, rhubarb, and cornstarch in a large bowl. Let stand, stirring occasionally, until the sugar is dissolved, about 10 minutes.

Pulse oats, brown sugar, flour, and cinnamon in a food processor or blender until well combined. Spoon fruit into ramekins and top with oat mixture.

Place ramekins on a foil lined baking sheet and bake in 400° oven for 25 to 30 minutes or until fruit is bubbling and topping is browned. Serve warm.

PREP TIME: 10 MINUTES  BAKE: 20-25 MINUTES

OVEN: 350° COOK: 10 MINUTES

1½ cups flour
1½ cups uncooked rolled oats
1 cup brown sugar
½ cup walnuts, finely chopped
¼ tsp. salt
¼ tsp. baking soda
1 cup butter, melted
1½ cups sugar
¼ cup water
2½ T corn starch
1 T vanilla
4 cups rhubarb, chopped

RHUBARB CRUNCH

MAKES 16 SERVINGS

Mix together flour, oats, brown sugar, nuts, salt, baking soda, and butter. Put ½ of mixture into a 9" x 13" cake pan.

In a large sauce pan; combine sugar, water, corn starch, and vanilla. Cook until clear. Add in rhubarb and continue to cook for 2 minutes or until it starts to soften. Pour rhubarb mixture over crust. Crumble remaining crust mixture over the top and bake at 350° for 20 to 25 minutes. Cool to warm and cut into squares and remove from pan.

CHIP KISSES

MAKES 3 DOZEN

PREP TIME: 30 MINUTES   BAKE: 25 MINUTES

OVEN: 300°

2 egg whites
⅛ tsp. salt
⅛ tsp. cream of tartar
½ cup sugar, sifted
1 cup semi-sweet chocolate morsels
¼ tsp. peppermint extract

Beat egg whites until foamy then add salt and cream of tartar. Continue beating until eggs are stiff enough to hold up in peaks but not dry. Add sugar 2 tablespoons at a time, beating thoroughly after each addition. Fold in chocolate chips and peppermint. Drop from teaspoons on ungreased parchment paper. Bake at 300° for 25 minutes. Remove from paper while slightly warm.

CHOCOLATE NUT COOKIES

MAKES 3 DOZEN

PREP TIME: 15 MINUTES   BAKE: 12 MINUTES

OVEN: 350°

1 12 oz. pkg. semi-sweet chocolate morsels
2 egg whites
dash of salt
½ cup sugar
½ tsp. vanilla
½ tsp. white vinegar
¾ cup walnuts, finely chopped

Melt chocolate chips; set aside. Beat egg whites with salt until foamy. Gradually add sugar 2 tablespoons at a time, beating until blended and stiff peaks form. Beat in vanilla and vinegar. Fold in melted chocolate and walnuts.

Drop heaping teaspoons of batter onto a greased cookie sheet. Bake at 350° for 12 minutes. Remove from cookie sheet to cool right away.

PREP TIME: *30 MINUTES*   BAKE: *12 MINUTES*
OVEN: *375°*   CHILL: *2 HOURS*

- 3 cups flour
- 1 tsp. baking soda
- ½ tsp. salt
- 1 cup butter, softened
- 1 cup sugar
- 2 6 oz. pkgs. solid chocolate mint wafers or thin cookies
- ½ cup brown sugar, firmly packed
- 2 eggs
- 2 T water
- 1 tsp. vanilla

MINT SURPRISE COOKIES

MAKES 3 DOZEN

Sift flour, salt, and baking soda together. In a separate bowl, cream the butter and sugars together. Add eggs, water, and vanilla. Add in dry ingredients and mix thoroughly. Cover and refrigerate for at least 2 hours. Roll dough to ⅛ inch thick, cut just larger than wafer. Enclose each chocolate wafer in dough pressing evenly over the wafer and around edge. Place on a greased baking sheet. Bake at 375° for 12 minutes.

PREP TIME: *30 MINUTES*   COOK: *12-14 MINUTES*
OVEN: *350°*

- 20 whole graham cracker squares
- 1 14 oz. can sweetened condensed milk
- 1 12 oz. pkg. semi-sweet chocolate morsels

QUICKIE CHOCOLATE CHIP COOKIES

MAKES 4 DOZEN

Crush or process graham crackers until very fine. Mix well with condensed milk. Add chocolate chips. Drop teaspoonfuls (1" diameter) onto a well-greased cookie sheet. Bake cookies at 350° for 12 to 14 minutes or until edges are lightly browned. Place cookies on rack immediately to cool.

DOUBLE CHOCOLATE REBELS

PREP TIME: 30 MINUTES

BAKE: 12 MINUTES

OVEN: 350°

1 cup sifted flour
½ tsp. baking soda
½ tsp. salt
6 T cocoa
1¼ cups butter, softened
1 tsp. vanilla extract
1½ cups sugar
1 egg, well beaten
¼ cup water
3 cups uncooked rolled oats
1 6 oz. pkg. semi-sweet
  chocolate morsels

MAKES 15 DOZEN

Sift together flour, baking soda, salt, and cocoa; set aside. Cream together butter and vanilla; Add sugar gradually, creaming until fluffy after each addition. Add the beaten egg in thirds beating thoroughly after each addition.

Add the dry ingredients to creamed mixture in two additions. Add water to the creamed mixture. Add the oats gradually, stirring well. Mix in the chocolate pieces. Drop teaspoons of mixture onto ungreased baking sheets. Bake at 350° for 12 minutes.

QUICK MIX SPRITZ

PREP TIME: 30 MINUTES

BAKE: 10-12 MINUTES

OVEN: 375°

2¼ cups flour
¾ cup sugar
¼ tsp. baking powder
½ tsp. salt
1 cup shortening
1 egg
1 tsp. vanilla extract

MAKES 5-6 DOZEN

Sift flour, sugar, baking powder, and salt together. Blend in shortening until mixture resembles pie crust. Add egg and vanilla extract; mix well. Put in cookie press and press cookies onto ungreased cookie sheet. Bake at 375° for 10 to 12 minutes. Place cookies on rack immediately to cool.

CHAPTER FIFTEEN

MORSELS & TIDBITS
BASIC COOKING & EQUIPMENT TIPS

BASIC COOKING TIPS

My advice for a novice cook is to develop basic cooking and knife skills, get familiar with seasonings, and learn common kitchen terminology. It will make the difference between a stressful and enjoyable cooking experience. The following basic cooking principles should help make your cooking go smoothly:

- Read the recipe from beginning to end before beginning.
- Have all ingredients out and measured before beginning.
- Have all utensils, bowls, pots, pans, and equipment out and ready when you need it.
- Keep your cutlery sharpened. A dull knife is dangerous and will slow prep time.
- Always preheat the oven.
- Recipes are guidelines. Switch it up a little with different herbs or similar ingredients. Cooking should be fun!

Many people are confused about the difference between kosher salt, sea salt, and table salt. Chemically there is little difference between all three, as all salts are at least 97.5% sodium chloride. Where they do differ is in their texture.

Table salt's fine granules dissolve quickly, making it the preferred salt of bakers. But be careful when using table salt. Because of its fine grain, one teaspoon of table salt contains more salt than one tablespoon of kosher or sea salt.

Kosher and sea salts have large, irregular granules that offer a briny taste and crunch when added to food at the last minute. Generally, savvy cooks tend to prefer kosher salt when cooking since its coarse texture is easier to take a pinch and control the amount added to dishes.

Salt is a flavor enhancer and preserver. Over seasoning your dish with salt can be disastrous if you are not familiar with the different types of salts. It is best to season your dish with a small amount at a time until you get the taste you like.

Seasoning food with black pepper takes a little getting used to, but don't worry, it's hard to screw up. Recipes are often vague calling for "freshly ground black pepper," "a sprinkle," "generously season," or "pepper to taste." Truth is there is not a lot of difference between them. It just takes a little time in the kitchen to get a feel for how much pepper you prefer in you food.

PEPPER GRINDER MATH—For those of you that own a pepper grinder but never know just how many cranks it takes to give you the desired amount of pepper (based on medium grind setting), here is a guide:

⅛ teaspoon = 5 full rotations
¼ teaspoon = 10 full rotations
½ teaspoon = 20 full rotations
1 teaspoon = 40 full rotations

KITCHEN EQUIPMENT TIPS

Like in any hobby or work that you do, it's important to have the right tools for the job. Equipping the kitchen with a few basic tools will make a big difference in the time and outcome of your recipe.

Selecting the right cutlery to use saves in prep time, makes a better presentation, and saves the aggravation from cutting with a wrong or dull knife. There is no need to buy expensive knife sets to properly equip a kitchen. A few essential pieces will accomplish most kitchen tasks. Here's a basic checklist:

- 6" TO 8" CHEF'S OR SANTOKU KNIFE: It's the most useful knife in the kitchen. Use it to chop or slice vegetables, meat, mince herbs, and garlic.
- 2" TO 4" PARING KNIFE: Good for paring fruit, cutting cheese, and mincing a small amount of herbs or garlic.
- 6" TO 12" SERRATED KNIFE: A must have knife to slice bread, bagels, meats, soft fruits, tomatoes, and melons.
- KITCHEN SHEARS: Select specially designed kitchen shears that come apart easily for cleaning. Kitchen shears are great

for snipping herbs, trimming fat off meat, cutting open packages, and snipping twine.

Never know which baking dish is the best to use? Here are a few tips to help with your decision:

- CERAMIC—Can go straight from the freezer to oven—even to the table, where it helps to keep food warm. It heats up gradually, so it is ideal for dishes that need slow, even cooking, such as custards and baked noodle dishes.
- GLASS—Like ceramic, glass is nonreactive, so it is good for acidic foods like tomatoes. Bakers like it because they can see if the bottom is done. It costs less than ceramic but can crack when exposed to big temperature swings.
- METAL—Metal heats quickly and gives food crisp edges, so it's perfect for cakes and brownies.

With the number of stovetop cookware options on the market, it is difficult to choose which one is best for your kitchen. All have their advantages so it really boils down to personal choice. Here are 5 things you should know to help you make an informed decision:

- HEAT CONDUCTIVITY: The better the heat conductivity, the more evenly food will cook. The quicker a pan reacts when the heat is adjusted up or down, the better. Some metals conduct heat better than others. Copper is a great heat conductor but is also difficult to maintain its beauty. Stainless does not conduct heat as well as others types of metal.
- PRICE: Cookware can be extremely expensive when you consider clad-style pans with two types of metal or the baked enamel brands. Stainless is fairly inexpensive. Buy the best you can afford.
- REACTIVITY: Tomatoes and other acidic foods can react to some metals and actually absorb the metal into the food. Some copper and aluminum pans, even non-stick coated aluminum, have a tendency to react to acidic dishes.

- MAINTENANCE: Copper and cast iron pans require the most work to maintain while stainless is likely the easiest to keep in good shape. Aluminum is easy to care for and a less expensive choice but can scratch and dent easily.

Whatever kind of cookware you decide to purchase, follow the manufacturer's recommendations for care. I recommend you start by buying one piece at a time rather than buying a full set that you may not use or are unhappy with.

When stove top cooking, here are a few rules of thumb to remember:

- Always preheat a pan at the temperature that you plan to cook at for about 1 minute before you begin to sauté, fry or sear. It will improve the cooking performance and help prevent sticking.
- Cold ingredients are much more likely to stick to a hot pan so allow refrigerated ingredients to set at room temperature for at least 15 minutes before cooking.
- Optimal cooking temperatures are from low to medium-high settings. Use high heat for boiling only.
- Select a burner that closely matches the diameter of the pan you plan to use.
- If you find that you need to add more oil when sautéing, browning, or frying, add it in a slow stream near the side of the pan. That way the oil is heated by the time it reaches the food.

Wood cutting boards are easy on the knife blade but have to be hand washed. Wood is also naturally porous so bacterial contamination from liquids and food can seep into the surface. Bamboo is a good alternative to wood. Still soft enough to be easy on the blade and it can be washed in the dishwasher. Wood cutting boards are best used for slicing breads and cheeses.

For a good utility cutting board, my preference is one made of compressed wood. They can be found in most kitchen stores and are available in many sizes, are sturdy, light weight, dishwasher safe and lasting.

A good rule of thumb is to select a cutting board 3 inches larger than your longest knife and replace the board when it develops an abundance of knife scars as bacteria can get trapped in them and grow.

CONFUSING KITCHEN TERMINOLOGY

Some people are confused by what minced, diced, and chopped actually look like. Here is a helpful visual aid that will give you an idea:

Minced   Diced   Chopped

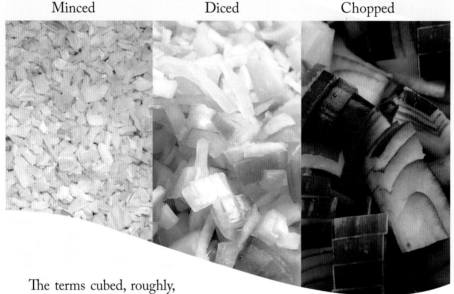

The terms cubed, roughly, or coarsely is just what it implies; large chunks or pieces. Don't take cooking too seriously and stress out about the exact size, but try to cut the ingredients uniformly. It will help the food cook evenly and make a better presentation.

Having a basic knowledge of cooking terminology will be helpful when learning how to cook. Here is a list of a few essential terms:

AL DENTE: Pasta or vegetables that are cooked until nearly done.

AU GRATIN: Oven baked dish topped with bread crumbs or cheese.

BASTE: The spooning or brushing of cooking liquid over the food.

BLANCH: To briefly plunge vegetables into boiling water.

BLEND: Stir ingredients using a large spoon in a circular motion.

BROWN: Quickly fry outside of meat leaving inside uncooked.

CREAM: To beat butter and sugar together until smooth.

DASH: Just less than ⅛ teaspoon.

DRAIN: Use a colander or sieve to separate liquid from food.

GREASE: Lightly coat dish with butter or oil to prevent sticking.

HEAPING: Ingredient rounded over the top of spoon or cup.

INFUSE: Allowing the flavors of the ingredients to blend.

LEVEL: Ingredient filled to top then leveled off with a straight edge.

MARINATE: Soaking meat in liquid ingredients to flavor or tenderize.

PINCH: As much as can be held between a thumb and index finger.

POACH: Where food is cooked on a stove top in a simmering liquid.

SAUTÉ: To quickly cook food in on a stove top with oil or butter.

SCANT: Just barely or slightly less than.

SKIM: Removing the fat or scum off the surface of a liquid.

SPLASH: 1 to 5 drops.

SOFT PEAK: Beaten egg white whose peak folds over when lifted.

STIFF PEAK: Beaten egg white whose peak holds when lifted.

WHISK: To beat rapidly with a wire whisk to increase fluffiness.

ZEST: The very outer surface of a citrus fruit.

CHICKEN COOKING TIMES

This chart provides approximate doneness times for fresh or thawed chicken, not frozen.

Type of Chicken	Weight	Roasting 350°F	Simmering	Grilling
Whole	3 to 4 lbs.	1¼ to 1½ hours	60 to 75 minutes	60 to 75 minutes
Breast Halves Bone-in	6 to 8 oz.	30 to 40 minutes	35 to 45 minutes	10 to 15 minutes each side
Breast Half Boneless	4 oz.	20 to 30 minutes	25 to 30 minutes	6 to 8 minutes each side
Legs or Thighs	4 to 8 oz.	40 to 50 minutes	40 to 50 minutes	10 to 15 minutes each side
Drumsticks	4 oz.	35 to 45 minutes	40 to 50 minutes	8 to 12 minutes each side
Wings or Winglets	2 to 3 oz.	30 to 40 minutes	35 to 45 minutes	8 to 12 minutes each side
Ground Meat	4 to 8 oz.	30 to 40 minutes	35 to 45 minutes	6 to 8 minutes each side

Poultry Storage Tips:

- WHOLE POULTRY can be stored in the freezer for up to 12 months.
- POULTRY PARTS can be stored in the freezer for up to 9 months.
- GROUND POULTRY can be stored in the freezer for up to 3 months.
- COOKED POULTRY can be refrozen for 3 to 4 months.
- THAWED POULTRY can be stored in the refrigerator 1–2 days.
- COOKED POULTRY can be stored in the refrigerator for 3–4 days.
- DOUBLE WRAPPING POULTRY before freezing will help hold in moisture.

TURKEY ROASTING TIMES

This is an approximate timetable for fresh or thawed turkey breast or whole turkey cooked at 325°F. Use a meat thermometer to assure the turkey reaches a minimum of 165°F in the innermost part of the thigh and the thickest part of the breast before removing from the oven.

WEIGHT (LBS.)	UN-STUFFED (HOURS)	STUFFED (HOURS)
4 to 6 breast	1½ to 2¼	n/a
6 to 8 breast	2¼ to 3¼	n/a
8 to 12 whole	2¾ to 3	3 to 3½
12 to 14 whole	3 to 3¾	3½ to 4
14 to 18 whole	3¾ to 4¼	4 to 4¼
18 to 20 whole	4¼ to 4½	4¼ to 4¾
20 to 24 whole	4½ to 5	4¾ to 5¼

Cooking times can be affected by shielding, stuffing, the depth of a roasting pan, temperature of the turkey, and oven temperature. The only way to be sure the turkey is fully cooked is to use a meat thermometer. —Dorothy Lane Market

Thawing a turkey in the refrigerator is the safest method. Expect 24 hours defrosting time for every 5 pounds of turkey. Keep the frozen turkey in the original wrapping and place it on a rack in the refrigerator to allow for air flow. Defrosting times may vary due to temperature settings of refrigerators.

Cold water thawing speeds up the defrosting process. Again, keep the frozen turkey in the original wrapping and place it in very cold water. Change the water every 30 minutes and allow about 30 minutes defrosting per pound of turkey. Cook immediately after thawing.

BEEF STEAK COOKING CHART

		Red-Hot Charcoal or Gas Grilling		Broiling 2" to 3" from Heat Source	
Thickness	Doneness	Side 1	Side 2	Side 1	Side 2
	Rare	4 mins.	2 mins.	5 mins.	4 mins.
	Medium	5 mins.	3 mins.	7 mins.	5 mins.
¾"	Well	7 mins.	5 mins.	10 mins.	8 mins.
	Rare	5 mins.	3 mins.	6 mins.	5 mins.
	Medium	6 mins.	4 mins.	8 mins.	6 mins.
1"	Well	8 mins.	6 mins.	11 mins.	9 mins.
	Rare	5 mins.	4 mins.	7 mins.	5 mins.
	Medium	7 mins.	5 mins.	8 mins.	7 mins.
1¼"	Well	9 mins.	7 mins.	12 mins.	10 mins.
	Rare	6 mins.	4 mins.	7 mins.	6 mins.
	Medium	7 mins.	6 mins.	9 mins.	7 mins.
1½"	Well	10 mins.	8 mins.	13 mins.	11 mins.
	Rare	7 mins.	5 mins.	8 mins.	7 mins.
	Medium	8 mins.	7 mins.	9 mins.	8 mins.
1¾"	Well	11 mins.	9 mins.	14 mins.	12 mins.

Cooking times are for fully thawed steaks. —Omaha Steaks

PORK
COOKING TIMES

METHOD	CUT	THICK/LBS.	COOKING TIME
ROASTING	Loin Roast, Bone-in or Boneless	2 to 5 lbs.	20 mins. per lb.
	Crown Roast	10 lbs.	12 mins. per lb.
	Tenderloin	½ to 1½ lbs.	20 to 27 mins. cooked at 450°
	Ribs	3 to 5 lbs.	1½ to 2 hours cooked at 350°
	Ham (Fully Cooked)	5 to 6 lbs.	20 mins. per lb.
BROILING OR GRILLING	Loin Chops Bone-in or Boneless	¾"	4 to 5 minutes each side
	Loin Chops Bone-in or Boneless	1½"	6 to 8 minutes each side
	Tenderloin	½ to 1½ lbs.	20 minutes
	Ground Patties	½"	4 to 5 minutes each side
SAUTÉING	Cutlets	¼"	2 minutes each side
	Loin Chops Bone-in or Boneless	¾"	4 to 5 minutes each side
	Tenderloin Medallions	¼" to ½"	2 to 4 minutes each side
	Ground Patties	½"	4 to 5 minutes each side
STEWING	Loin or Shoulder	1" cubes	1½ to 2 hours

FISH COOKING TIMES

BAKED FISH

PORTION	OVEN TEMP	WEIGHT	COOK TIME
Whole	350°	3 to 5 lbs.	25 to 30 mins.
Filets	350°	3 to 5 lbs.	25 to 30 mins.
Steaks	350°	3 to 5 lbs.	35 to 40 mins.

PAN FRIED FISH

PORTION	COOK TEMP.	THICKNESS	COOK TIME
Whole	Medium	2" to 4"	8 – 15 mins.
Filets	Medium	¾"	7 – 9 mins.
Steaks	Medium	1"	9 – 10 mins.

GRILLED FISH
(4" FROM HEAT SOURCE)

PORTION	COOK TEMP.	THICKNESS	COOK TIME
Whole	Medium	2" to 4"	10 – 20 mins.
Filets	Medium	¾"	7 – 9 mins.
Steaks	Medium	1"	9 – 10 mins.

STEAMING FISH
(OVER GENTLY BOILING WATER)

PORTION	COOK TEMP.	THICKNESS	COOK TIME
Whole	Gentle Boil	2" to 4"	10 – 12 mins.
Filets	Gentle Boil	¾"	10 – 12 mins.
Steaks	Gentle Boil	1"	10 – 15 mins.

POACHING FISH
(IN SIMMERING LIQUID)

PORTION	COOK TEMP.	THICKNESS	COOK TIME
Whole	Gentle Simmer	2" to 4"	8 – 10 mins.
Filets	Gentle Simmer	¾"	6 – 8 mins.
Steaks	Gentle Simmer	1"	6 – 8 mins.

EXPERIMENTING WITH HERBS AND SPICES

HERB	SUGGESTED USES
Basil	Fish, lamb, ground meats, stews, salads, soups, sauces.
Chives	Salads, sauces, soups, veal, pork, chicken, turkey, vegetables.
Cumin	Lamb, pork, chilis, stews, lentils, rice, couscous.
Curry Powder	Lamb, veal, chicken, fish, tomatoes, tomato soup, mayonnaise.
Dill	Lamb, beef, chicken, fish, fish sauces, soups, salads, tomatoes, cabbages, carrots, cauliflower, cucumbers, macaroni, potatoes, green beans.
Garlic Powder	Beef, chicken, lamb, veal, pork, fish, soups, salads, vegetables, tomatoes, potatoes.
Onion Powder	Beef, veal, pork, chicken, turkey, stews, vegetables, soups, salads.
Oregano	Mediterranean dishes, tomato-based sauces and stews, ground meats, lamb, artichokes, potatoes.
Paprika	Beef, chicken, lamb, veal, pork, fish, soups, salads, sauces, vegetables.
Rosemary	Chicken, meatloaf, beef, lamb, pork, mushrooms, sauces, stuffing, potatoes, peas, lima beans.
Sage	Veal, pork, chicken, turkey, fish, stews, biscuits, tomatoes, green beans, lima beans, onions.
Thyme	Veal, pork, chicken, turkey, mushrooms, sauces, soups, onions, peas, tomatoes, salads.

1 tablespoon of fresh herbs = 1 teaspoon of dried.

INGREDIENT EQUIVALENTS

APPLE: 1 medium = 1 cup sliced

ASPARAGUS: 1 bunch = 2 cups

BACON: 1 strip cooked = 2 T crumbled

BANANA: 1 medium = ⅓ cup mashed

BEANS & PEAS: 1 lb. or 2½ cups = 6 cups cooked

BELL PEPPER: 1 medium = 1⅓ cup

BREAD: 5 slices = 1 cup of crumbs

BROCCOLI: 1 head = 3½ cups florets

CABBAGE: 1 small head = 5 – 6 cups shredded

CARROT: 1 medium = ⅔ cup diced

CAULIFLOWER: 1 head = 3¾ cups florets

CELERY: 1 stalk = ½ cup diced

CHEESE: American or cheddar, 4 oz. = 1 cup shredded

CHERRIES, RED: 1 lb. = 2 cups pitted

CHOCOLATE: chips 6 oz. pkg. = 1 cup

CHOCOLATE: unsweetened, 8 oz. pkg. = 8 squares (1 oz. each)

CREAM CHEESE: 8 oz. pkg. = 1 cup

CREAM: whipping, ½ pint (1 cup) = 2 cups whipped

GARLIC: 1 clove = 1 tsp. minced

GRAHAM CRACKER: 14 squares = 1 cup finely crushed

GREEN BEANS: 1 lb. or 3 cups = 2½ cups cooked

GREEN ONION: 1 medium = ¼ cup minced

JALAPEÑO: 1 medium = 2 T minced

LEMON: fresh juice, 1 medium lemon = 3 T

LEMON: fresh zest, 1 medium lemon = 2 tsp.

LIME: fresh juice, 1 medium lime = 3 T

LIME: fresh zest, 1 medium lime = 2 tsp.

MACARONI: 1 cup = 2½ cooked

MUSHROOMS: 1 cup = 2 oz. 1 large mushroom = ¼ cup sliced

NUTS: 1 cup finely chopped = 4 oz. pkg.

ONION, COOKING: 1 medium = ½ cup chopped

ONION, COOKING: 1 large = 1 cup chopped

ONION, RED: 1 large = 2 cups chopped

ORANGE: fresh juice 1 medium orange= ⅓ to ½ cup

ORANGE: fresh zest, 1 medium orange = 1 to 2 T

POPCORN: ¼ cup = 5 cups popped

POTATO, RUSSET: 1 medium = ⅔ cup diced, ½ cup mashed

POTATO, RED: 1 medium = ½ cup diced

POTATO, YUKON: 1 medium = ¾ cup diced

RHUBARB: 1 lb. or 4 cups = 2 cups cooked

RICE LONG GRAIN: 1 cup = 3 cups cooked

RICE QUICK COOK: 1 cup = 2 cups cooked

SALTINE CRACKERS: 28 squares = 1 cup finely crushed

SPAGHETTI: 8 oz. pkg. = 4 cups

SPINACH: 1 lb. or 12 cups = 1½ cups cooked

SWEET POTATO: 1 medium = 1 cup diced

VANILLA WAFERS: 22 cookies = 1 cup finely crushed

TOMATOES: 1 medium = ½ cup cooked

ZUCCHINI: 1 medium = 1½ cups sliced

TIP: *Before and after preparations amounts are approximations and may vary.*

LIQUID EQUIVALENT CHART

CUP	OUNCE	TABLESPOON	TEASPOON	MILLILITER
1/16	1/2	1	3	15
1/8	1	2	6	30
1/4	2	4	12	60
1/3	3	5	16	80
1/2	4	8	24	120
2/3	5	11	32	160
3/4	6	12	36	180
1	8	16	48	240

1 cup	=	8 oz.	=	½ pint
2 cups	=	16 oz.	=	1 pint
4 cups	=	32 oz.	=	2 pints
2 pints	=	1 quart		
8 pints	=	4 quarts		
4 quarts	=	1 gallon		

REFERENCES

"10 Fun Facts About Chocolate." *About A Mom*. N.p., n.d. Web. 27 June 2013.

"10 Tips for Making the Perfect Souffle." *About.com British & Irish Food*. N.p., n.d. Web. 27 June 2013.

"12 Facts About Lima Beans." *12 Facts About Lima Beans*. N.p., n.d. Web. 20 June 2013.

"About AmarettoÂ Liqueur." *About.com Home Cooking*. N.p., n.d. Web. 01 Aug. 2012. http://homecooking.about.com/od/alcohol/a/whatisamaretto.htm.

"Answer to Different Grades of Ground Beef." *Answer to Different Grades of Ground Beef*. N.p., n.d. Web. 11 Mar. 2013.

"Basic Kitchen Checklist." *About.com Cooking Equipment*. N.p., n.d. Web. 03 Sept. 2013.

Breakfast - The Most Important Meal of the Day." *Breakfast - The Most Important Meal of the Day*. N.p., n.d. Web. 18 Apr. 2013.

"Beating Egg Whites Tips and Hints." *About.com Home Cooking*. N.p., n.d. Web. 21 June 2013.

"Buffalo Wing." *Wikipedia*. Wikimedia Foundation, 08 Jan. 2012. Web. 01 Aug. 2012. http://en.wikipedia.org/wiki/Buffalo wing.

"Cabbage Nutrition Facts and Health Benefits." *Nutrition And You.com*. N.p., n.d. Web. 14 Aug. 2013.

"Cherry Fruit Nutrition Facts and Health Benefits." *Nutrition And You.com*. N.p., n.d. Web. 22 Aug. 2013.

"Chicken Handling, Safety & Storage." *RecipeTips.com*. N.p., n.d. Web. 04 Sept. 2013.

Chip. "Measuring Freshly Ground Black Pepper | Cookthink." *Measuring Freshly Ground Black Pepper | Cookthink*. N.p., n.d. Web. 27 Oct. 2012.http://www.cookthink.com/reference/211/Measuring_freshly_ground_black_pepper.

"Choose the Best Apple." —*How to Cooking Tips*. N.p., n.d. Web. 05 Apr. 2013.

"Common Ingredient Substitutions." *Allrecipes.com*. N.p., n.d. Web. 26 Sept. 2013.

"Conversions and Equivalents." *Cooking at Home with The Culinary Institute of America*. Hoboken: John Wiley & Sons, 2003. 292-96. Print.

"Cooking Meat? Check the New Recommended Temperatures." *Home*. N.p., n.d. Web. 14 Aug. 2013.

"Cooking Terminology—Understanding Culinary Terms." *Cooking Terminology*. N.p., n.d. Web. 26 Sept. 2013.

Davis, Sarah. "Difference Between Ground Beef & Ground Round." *EHow*. Demand Media, 03 Mar. 2011. Web. 11 Mar. 2013.

"Difference between Hollandaise & BÃ©arnaise (Bearnaise)." N.p., n.d. Web. 15 Oct. 2012. <http://www.ochef.com/815.htm>.

"Frango." *Wikipedia*.Wikimedia Foundation, 27 Apr. 2013. Web. 27 June 2013.

"Facts About Cherries." *Facts About Cherries*. N.p., n.d. Web. 22 Aug. 2013.

"Fish Cooking Times." *RecipeTips.com*. N.p., n.d. Web. 04 Sept. 2013.

Forrest Gump. Dir. Robert Zemeckis. By Eric Roth. Perf. Tom Hanks, Robin Wright, Gary Sinise, Sally Field, and Mykelti Williamson. Paramount Pictures, 1994. Film.

"Fun Chocolate Facts." *Fun Chocolate Facts*. N.p., n.d. Web. 27 June 2013.

Grotto, David W. *101 Foods That Could save Your Life!* New York: Bantam, 2008. Print.

"** Hangover Cure? How to Treat a Hangover **." *** Hangover Cure? How to Treat a Hangover **. N.p., n.d. Web. 18 Apr. 2013.

"History." *Lea & PerrinsÂ®*. N.p., n.d. Web. 15 Oct. 2012. <http://www.leaperrins.com/history.aspx>.

"How To Choose and Buy Cookware, Guide to Choosing Cookware, Choosing Pots and Pans." *How To Choose and Buy Cookware, Guide to Choosing Cookware, Choosing Pots and Pans*. N.p., n.d. Web. 27 Sept. 2013.

"How to Cure a Hangover." *LoveToKnow*. N.p., n.d. Web. 18 Apr. 2013.

"How To Pick a PotatoHome Hacks." *The Kitchn*. N.p., n.d. Web. 11 Mar. 2013.

"How To: Simplify." *: {Tips & Tricks} Peeling Pearl Onions*. N.p., n.d. Web. 12 Sept. 2012. http://www.howto-simplify.com/2011/02/tips-tricks-peeling-pearl-onions.html.

"Island Ireland: Irish Blessings & Prayers." *Island Ireland: Irish Blessings & Prayers*. N.p., n.d. Web. 21 Aug. 2012. http://islandireland.com/Pages/folk/sets/bless.html.

"Kosher vs. Table vs. Sea Salts." *: Recipes and Cooking : Food Network*. N.p., n.d. Web. 27 Oct. 2012. http://www.foodnetwork.com/recipes-and-cooking/kosher-vs-table-vs-sea-salts/index.html.

"Letting Meat Rest After Cooking—The Virtual Weber Bullet." *Letting Meat Rest After Cooking—The Virtual Weber Bullet*. N.p., n.d. Web. 11 July 2013.

"Liquid Smoke." *Wikipedia*. Wikimedia Foundation, 30 July 2012. Web. 01 Aug. 2012. http://en.wikipedia.org/wiki/Liquid_smoke.

"Mashed PotatoÂ Selection." *About.com Home Cooking*. N.p., n.d. Web. 11 Mar. 2013.

Mateljan, George. *The World's Healthiest Foods: Essential Guide for the Healthiest Way of Eating*. Seattle, WA: George Mateljan Foundation, 2006. Print.

Molina, Marcia. "Italian Stewed Tomatoes." *Allrecipes.com*. N.p., n.d. Web. 11 June 2013.

Norton, Kim. "Wood Vs. Plastic Cutting Boards & Bacteria | EHow." *EHow*. Demand Media, 25 May 2010. Web. 04 Sept. 2013.

"Potluck." *Wikipedia*. Wikimedia Foundation, 31 Dec. 2012. Web. 07 Jan. 2013.

"Preparing a Turkey—Turkey Preparation." *RecipeTips.com*. N.p., n.d. Web. 05 Sept. 2013.

Quinlan, Christine. "Bakeware Basic Training." *Food & Wine* Nov (2010): 129. Print.

"Shoo Fly, Don't Bother Me." *Wikipedia*. Wikimedia Foundation, 06 June 2013. Web. 27 June 2013.

"Soggy Dollar Bar." *Soggy Dollar Bar*. N.p., n.d. Web. 01 Aug. 2012. http://www.soggydollar.com/soggy-dollar-bar/default.aspx.

"SOURDOUGH." *Food Facts & Trivia: Sourdough*. N.p., n.d. Web. 07 Jan. 2013. *WiseGeek*. Conjecture, n.d. Web. 07 Jan. 2013.

"The Big Thaw—Safe Defrosting Methods for Consumers." *The Big Thaw - Safe Defrosting Methods for Consumers*. N.p., n.d. Web. 11 June 2013.

"Today's Pork: Cooking Times and Temperatures." *Pork Cooking Time Chart*. N.p., n.d. Web. 05 Sept. 2013.

"U.S. Apple Association." *U.S. Apple Association*. N.p., 23 Dec. 2010. Web. 01 Aug. 2012. <http://usapple.org/>.

"What's the Difference between Ground Beef and Ground Chuck?" *Yahoo! Answers*. Yahoo!, n.d. Web. 11 Mar. 2013.

"Why Breakfast Is The Most Important Meal Of The Day Food Science." *The Kitchn*.com N.p., n.d. Web. 18 Apr. 2013.

"Yankee Doodle." *Wikipedia*. Wikimedia Foundation, 25 Feb. 2013. Web. 26 Feb. 2013.

"Yankee Doodle Historical Period: The American Revolution, 1763-1783." *Yankee Doodle*. N.p., n.d. Web. 26 Feb. 2013.

RECIPE INDEX

TECHNIQUES, TIPS, & INFORMATIONAL INDEX